SCHOOL MANAGEMENT SKILLS

SCHOOL MANAGEMENT SKILLS

edited by

MICHAEL MARLAND

Headteacher, North Westminster Community School, London

Honorary Professor of Education, Warwick University

with contributions by:

Colin Bayne-Jardine
Keith Blackburn
Lesley Bulman
Jack Dunham
Laurie Goodhand
Ian Leslie
Robert McCormick
George Phipson

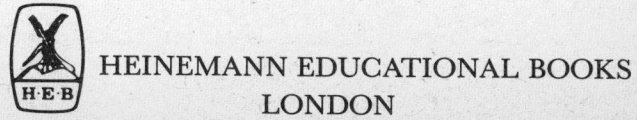

HEINEMANN EDUCATIONAL BOOKS
LONDON

Heinemann Educational Books Ltd
22 Bedford Square, London WC1B 3HH

LONDON EDINBURGH MELBOURNE AUCKLAND
HONG KONG SINGAPORE KUALA LUMPUR
NEW DELHI IBADAN NAIROBI JOHANNESBURG
PORTSMOUTH (NH) KINGSTON

First published 1986

British Library Cataloguing in Publication Data
School management skills. – Heinemann
   organization in schools series)
   1. School management and organization – Great
   Britain
   I. Marland, Michael   II. Bayne-Jardine, Colin
   371.2'00941   LB2901

ISBN 0–435–80594–0

Phototypesetting by Georgia Origination, Liverpool
Printed and bound in Great Britain by
Biddles Ltd, Guildford and King's Lynn

Contents

Preface

The Heinemann *Organization in Schools Series* is a systematic and wide-ranging attempt to help those working in schools to improve the planning and management and thus the quality of schooling by a methodical study of the ways in which schools can be organized. The books relate theory to practice in the belief that the one illuminates the other and that the management of a particular school is much improved if it is rooted not only in the knowledge of that area, those pupils, and that school, but also in an understanding of the ideas, observation, experience, and research of others.

The majority of books in the series have focused on a section of education: primary, middle, secondary, or sixth form. This, however, addresses itself to skills needed in *all* schools, and should be of value to responsibility holders in primary schools as much as to pastoral heads and heads of departments in secondary schools.

Michael Marland

Introduction

Michael Marland

Our schools are unique throughout the world in the extent to which planning decisions of all sorts, from curriculum to organization, are located in the schools themselves. For those of us working in schools, it is true, the day-to-day feeling is more likely to be of the burden of external constraints which local education authority procedures, budgets and outside pressures put upon us. Paradoxically, though, we feel these restraints only because of the very great freedom and the expectation that this engenders. In a USA school, for instance, a 'Principal' is not only called an 'administrator' but his/her task is very much to carry out the policies developed by the School Board. In England and Wales, despite some recent centralist tendencies, a significant proportion of the key decisions are made within the school, often by teachers who hold 'posts of responsibility'. This elevates the management skills of teachers, as opposed to their purely pedagogical skills, into very great importance. Indeed, in no education system in the world are the skills of school management within the schools so important.

However, our initial training and much in-service training pays little regard to the fact that teaching is, from this perspective, a life-time of professional collaboration over in-school management in which a large proportion of time and energy is spent jointly reviewing, analysing, speculating, planning and implementing. As much in a primary school as a secondary, the moment a teacher accepts a 'post of responsibility', his/her prime professional task is the leadership of other professionals. Although the primary responsibility holder or the secondary team leader (whether head of house or head of year) will spend more of the week working directly with pupils, his/her greatest worries, stresses and achievements will be the management of others. There is ample evidence that teachers find it difficult to exercise this responsibility. For instance, of the

1

primary school, HMI remark:

> In a quarter of the schools in the survey teachers with positions of curricular
> or organisational responsibility were having a noticeable influence on the
> quality of work in the school as a whole. In the remaining schools there was
> little evidence that the influence of teachers with curricular responsibilities
> spread beyond the work in their own classes. (DES 1978, p. 37)

and of the secondary school:

> The claim that schools are over-managed and that teachers are spending too
> much time on duties other than teaching was not supported by the evidence
> of the survey. Indeed, in most schools teachers with posts of special
> responsibility for the teaching of particular subjects or for the social and
> pastoral care of pupils were allocated few additional non-teaching periods
> and often had insufficient time to carry out fully those duties which could
> only be performed when the pupils were present. (DES 1979, p. 65)

Jack Dunham, in Chapter 7, gives evidence from another
perspective of the stresses felt by many with school management
responsibilities. And any consideration of the curriculum of most
schools reveals the difficulties of in-school curriculum planning (for
example, DES 1981, p. 72):

> The attempt to move towards establishing a coherent and fully thought out
> model of the curriculum – whether that of the Red Book or any other – is
> less comfortable than looking at existing subjects on a timetable and
> conjuring with time allocations; the process is time-consuming and often
> frustrating.

There is now a considerable literature on school management,
together with an excellent association devoted to this aspect of
education: The British Educational Management and
Administration Society. The Open University courses have been of
assistance to many who have been able to take them, and have
produced course books which have valuable case studies as well as
theoretical background and some detailed task analysis (OU 1981).
Much of the interesting work, however, has been concerned with
structure and broad managerial approaches. In the meantime the
ordinary responsibility holder is faced with specific professional
demands which simply cannot be learned from experience as a
teacher of pupils in a classroom. The demands of teaching will have
developed valuable skills. The invention, planning, preparation of
learning material, building of relationships and group management,
for instance, learned in class teaching are all valuable components of
responsibility posts in school management, but the use, construction
and context are very different when the responsibility is for other
adults.

Not only is there comparatively little to read to help you on how to
carry out school management tasks (the 'Further Reading' section
on page 127 gives a selection), but there are too few in-service courses,
especially short courses concentrating on specific tasks. A few LEAs

run excellent courses, such as the Inner London Education Authority middle-management courses, but throughout our whole education system there is almost a conspiracy of silence about how people do the tasks of school management. It is thought obligatory to be against 'tips for teachers' in a form of academic snobbery, and speaker after speaker and writer after writer refuse to explain or tell for fear of appearing omni-competent or a know-all. This book, therefore, is planned to help the teacher who in some way or other is taking part in the management of a school, small or large. Certain skills are used in a variety of posts. They can be prepared for, and ways found of relating existing experience, knowledge and skills to the tasks of school management.

The selection of eight aspects of skills in this volume is only a modest one, including some of those the responsibility holder is most likely to need to develop. In each case the writer, speaking from personal experience as well as research study, endeavours to set the task in the wider context of the education system and the needs of the school. The writers have tried to be as precise as possible in giving guidance to help teachers develop their ability to cope successfully with the tasks.

In all such management and leadership, of course, there is a mingling of an individual's personal qualities with his/her professional skills. Implicit or explicit throughout the eight chapters is the fact that mere 'skills' are insufficient. School management requires intelligence, imagination, energy, warmth of personality, humility, and persistence. These and other human qualities can probably not be learned from books, but many aspects of the tasks can be thought out in advance and the skills prepared for.

References

DES (1978) *Primary Education in England*. HMSO.
DES (1979) *Aspects of Secondary Education in England*. HMSO.
DES (1981) *The Curriculum 11-16: a Review of Progress*. HMSO.
OPEN UNIVERSITY (1981) *Management and the School*. Milton Keynes: Open University Press.

1   Planning Discussion

Laurie Goodhand

One of the most common and valuable steps in school management is the prepara-
tion of a 'discussion document'. A request to prepare one can daunt many even
experienced teachers. The fear of failing keeps many out of the process. The poor
quality of some such documents hinders school discussion and planning.

Reviewing, evaluating and considering plans is a central management task,
and one in which most of a school's staff can and should take part. This first
chapter, therefore, focuses on the discussion document as the enabling device for
planning. Laurie Goodhand sets the document itself in the context of a typical
planning structure within a fairly large school. The essence of the procedure is, of
course, the same in any school.

MM

This chapter argues the case for the involvement of a well informed
staff in a participatory decision-making process. Discussion documents occupy a central role in this process. Many of these documents should be concerned with the continuous review and evaluation of the school work, and they should involve all teachers, along
with members of other groups associated with the school. Most
important issues will surface from such documents. Much of the
information related to major school issues should be routinely available within the school through systematic means of collecting and
using data and through in-service training programmes. The final
section of the chapter takes the reader through the process of
preparing and using a discussion document.

The need for planning

Most teachers are aware of the haphazard nature of decision-making
that occurs in some schools. Some poor decisions affect only one area
of a school (for example, a departmental or pastoral team); others

affect the whole school and all of its students. Bad decisions usually arise either from a lack of awareness of or response to an issue or problem, or from an uninformed or undemocratic decision-making process. Decision-making in schools needs to be well informed, carefully considered and participatory. One of the key strategies to involve staff in the decision-making process in a school is the careful use of discussion documents.

The case for discussion documents

Recent years have seen increased change and innovation in schools. All the indications are that the rate of change in society and its technology (and the implications for education) will continue to accelerate. There will be more decisions for schools to take in response to these changes; there will be more policy initiatives, more curriculum changes to review and to evaluate. There will therefore be an increased need for good discussion documents, the benefits of which can be summarized as follows:
1 Good decision-making needs well informed decision-makers
2 Implementation of policy needs carefully considered planning based on a full knowledge of facts, possible advantages and disadvantages
3 Goodwill and a participative response occur when staff have been part of the decision-making process and understand fully the reasons for a decision
4 A well informed staff, teaching and non-teaching, is able to respond to all issues within the total context of an institution, its philosophy, values and policies, and is able to participate in educational debate
5 A well informed staff educates its managers
6 Teachers are encouraged to evaluate change and to devise strategies to carry out the evaluation; the teacher becomes a teacher-researcher
7 The professional development and promotion prospects of all staff are enhanced; there is a heightened awareness of the needs for in-service training.

The decision-making process

Discussion documents are part of a decision-making process within a school. Institutions tend to operate successfully when there is a clear management policy on how decisions are made and implemented. This policy needs to be understood by all the staff. It should also incorporate the following points:
1 How priorities for discussion and policy-making are determined

2 How membership of a working group is determined (a working group may be part of a department or pastoral team, a pre-existing school working party, or a newly-constituted working party)
3 What access the working group has to finances, in-service training time, resources, etc.
4 To whom the working group is accountable in the first instance (for example, head of year, senior management, staff meeting)
5 When the working group will make interim and final recommendations
6 How the working group will report its findings and recommendations
7 How final decisions are made within the school
8 Who is responsible for oversight and review of the implementation of any decision.

Although the headteacher is directly responsible for the management of the school, a democratic decision-making process has the benefits of staff awareness, participation and commitment. One model which has worked with a fair amount of success in one ILEA school is shown in diagrammatic form in Figure 1.1.

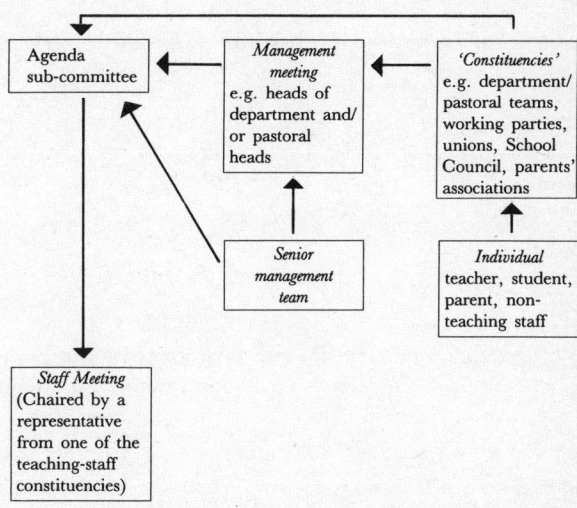

Figure 1.1   A model of how issues are raised in one school

Any individual may raise an issue, area of concern or proposed policy in a meeting of their own constituency (for example, subject department, parent–teacher association, working party, etc.). That constituency may decide that the area is one which concerns, or has implications for, the whole school, and may either refer it directly to the agenda sub-committee, or to a management meeting of heads of department and/or pastoral heads. The agenda sub-committee meets well in advance of staff meetings and considers all items submitted to it. For each item raised, the agenda sub-committee has a variety of options. It can decide to:

1 Refer back to constituency (either because the item has not been debated at the constituency level or because the constituency alone is concerned with the area and any decisions reached)
2 Pass on to staff meeting as a matter of information only
3 Pass on to staff meeting for a decision to be made
4 Pass on to staff meeting for initial presentation, and then for discussion in various constituencies, or in a working party, before coming back to the staff meeting.

The agenda sub-committee will also decide on the order of the agenda, the time allotted for presentation and/or discussion, and the need for the documentation to be distributed prior to the meeting.

Once a policy decision has been made at a staff meeting, it *may* be passed back to a management meeting to decide on the implementation, timing and evaluation – although the staff meeting may make recommendations on these.

Clearly most items for decision in a school do not have to pass through this whole process; many are resolved at the subject department or pastoral team level, but the same kinds of procedure apply.

In decision-making models similar to the one described, a discussion document may be produced at various stages:

1 From individuals to their constituency
2 From constituency to staff meeting (at the request of the agenda sub-committee)
3 From working party, or other constituency, to staff as a working paper, or to raise awareness
4 From working party as final report to staff meeting.

Some examples of the need for discussion documents

Here are seven examples of changes or reviews where a discussion document would seem to be necessary to guide decision-making. I have indicated after each example the groups in school who would be concerned directly or indirectly in the decision made:

1 Arguing the case for a pollution unit in a second-year science course. (Departmental course-planning team directly; other departments with curriculum overlap on this particular area.)
2 Introducing a new A-level syllabus for English. (English department only, unless the syllabus introduces radical changes in assessment, course work demands, etc.)

3 Review of the option scheme for the fourth year in a mixed secondary school. (Working group; separate department/pastoral team; whole staff.)
4 Developing a whole-school policy on multicultural education. (Working group; separate department/pastoral teams; whole staff.)
5 Review of the lower school home economics course. (Department team; liaison with feeder primary school and departments with curriculum overlap.)
6 Developing a reading policy in a primary school. (Whole staff; liaison with secondary schools.)
7 Reviewing the reception of the new intake into the secondary school. (Pastoral team with primary teachers; whole staff of secondary and primary schools.)

Other groups involved in decision-making

The examples above and the routes in Figure 1.1 appear to omit certain key groups who are significantly affected by, or interested in, changes in a school. Governors (or managers) have oversight of the curriculum. Well informed governors can bring various benefits to the school – for example, expertise from outside the immediate world of education; pressure on local authorities for necessary resourcing; contact between the school and the community. Interested governors should certainly receive discussion documents and/or join working parties. It is a valuable experience for governors to be involved in the *process* of how decisions and policies are arrived at, rather than just to act as recipients of final policy decisions. A good governing body can also act as an effective bridge between the school and the local community: they may be able to convey the opinions of parents and local employers to the school, and also explain to parents and employers the school's philosophies, educational aims and methods of working.

Parental involvement in working groups, in writing discussion documents, and in establishing school policies is very rare. However, if parents *and* students are involved in working parties and in writing discussion documents, there is likely to be, for example, more understanding of and support for the educational ideas behind curriculum development.

Student involvement in working groups has proved very effective in the school referred to earlier. The School Council is one of the constituencies which can attend and raise items at staff meetings. As the direct recipients of education, they have had a lot to offer the school. They have spoken at and prepared documents for staff meetings on using talk/discussion in the classroom; the demands of examination course-work; and racism in the school. They have joined in working parties (for example, on sexual differentiation, multicultural and anti-racist education), staff conferences and course-planning meetings.

There is a welcome movement towards 'community schools', and a curriculum concerned with the local community, and learning that values the experiences students bring with them into school. Even though ultimate curriculum decisions may be made inside these schools, there should be considerable involvement in the decision-making process by members of the local communities, which include students.

Where do issues come from?

The issue or problem may arise from a wide variety of sources, for example:
1 Request from governors/LEA to develop and implement a policy
2 Parental/governor's complaint
3 Staff unrest or revolution
4 Student unrest or revolution
5 Inspired senior management (ideas plucked from the air!) HMI or local authority inspection of school.
Apart from the first example, nearly all issues and problems should be more readily identified, focused and dealt with through *a process of continuous review and evaluation*.

Review and evaluation documents

One way of achieving this continuous review is for each subject department to carry out a regular moderation and evaluation of all its courses. This might be done once a term or once a year. Such moderation/evaluation exercises are only successful if the department has agreed on the *criteria* by which it will judge the success of its courses. These criteria might describe competences at various skills and processes; social interactions and observed behaviour; understanding of concepts, etc. A pastoral team should also meet to evaluate its work over a period of time.

This continuous process of evaluation is more likely to be effective if it is a *whole-school policy* and if there are agreed guidelines for the evaluation. Each department (or pastoral team or working party) is effectively evaluating for itself in the first instance. It is being self-critical in terms of evidence that the department has itself collected. It is making recommendations for areas or issues to be considered in the future. Some of these issues may be identified as departmental or pastoral concerns; some may have more far-reaching implications. The product of this evaluation process is most usefully expressed as a written *review report*. The review report is a document which arises from staff discussion concerned with the evaluation of a team's work and which leads to further staff discussion arising from its recommendations, criticisms and plaudits. Effective review reports will be succinct and to the point; their writers need precise guidelines, examples of which are given below (Figures 1.2 and 1.3).

Keeping the school under review

1   At the end of each school year every course in years 1–5 is the subject of a review report. The purpose of these reports is to draw together in one report all the various influences on learning as they affect individual courses.

2   The reports, written by heads of department and/or course coordinators, review the following:
  (a) Course aims
  (b) Course planning
  (c) Assessment and record-keeping procedures
  (d) The moderation process and findings
  (e) Course evaluation
  (f) Action to be taken to modify the course for the following year
  (g) How school policies on support for learning across the curriculum have affected the course (working parties, social education induction programmes, cooperation with other departments/courses)
  (h) Examination entries and last year's results
  (i) Timetable allocations, finance, staffing and other resource needs.

3   Writing the reports is intended to help clarify thinking on how the course is being taught and can be improved. The reports are collectively an important way in which we communicate with colleagues, governors and LEA inspectors.

Figure 1.2

End of year review

At the end of each year, the head of year draws together the work of the year under the following headings:
  Critical incidents of the year
  Resources and rooms
  Timetable
  Year council
  Year activities (for example, trips, fund-raising)
  Work with tutors
  Outside agencies
  Social education programme
  Use of on-site study centre provision
  The curriculum
  Summary of issues, problems and successes on a form-by-form basis
  Work with departments, including learning support
  Recommendations and plans for next year.

Figure 1.3

Individual review reports may determine issues and priorities for a particular team, but the collection of review reports can help to determine wider issues for a faculty head or senior management team. It is because these review reports have the potential of 'throwing up' wider issues, that they should have a fairly standard format. It is easy to see how the issues cited on pages 8 and 9 might have arisen from an individual review report or from a collection of such reports. One major advantage of a review report system is that it involves all staff in the curriculum process, either directly in writing a report, or by attendance at a moderation or review meeting. A second major advantage is that the issues arise directly from an assessment of students' work and attitudes, and from an evaluation involving the teachers concerned. My earlier comments indicate that students' and parents' views should have some place in the review reports, and therefore that students and parents should have some involvement in the review and evaluation process. This might be achieved by representation at review meetings, through student and parent comment pages in subject exercise books or folders, and through a systematic attempt to use parents' report evenings (or PTAs) to gain feedback.

The essential point is that a process of review and evaluation aids all levels of management in clearly identifying the real issues. It gives management responsibility to those directly involved with areas of the curriculum. It throws up answers to questions such as 'Whose problem is it?'; 'Who should prepare a paper on this?'; 'To which audience?'; 'Who should be taking action?'. It should enable schools to avoid the panic issues – for example, 'What is the senior management team going to do about . . . homework standards/discipline/poor examination results/mixed-ability teaching/ the wearing of jewellery(!)?' – the emotive speeches at emergency staff meetings, and the inevitable hasty decision.

How schools collect information

The writers of school discussion documents already have a full-time job. They certainly will not have time to research and write another Bullock Report, and if they did, the rest of the staff would not have the time or inclination to read it. On the other hand if the document is produced as one side of barely legible A4 dashed off while 4C do silent reading, it may well be read but it is hardly likely to add much to the collective wisdom of the staffroom. However, there is a middle way between these two extremes. It does assume that staff are well informed and that, on most issues, it should not be necessary to educate staff from a position of zero knowledge. The school's organization needs to ensure that:
1 The task of collecting information is shared widely

2 There is a continuous process of information collection and dissemination.

The various levels of management groups in a school (including working parties) should use some (or all) of the following strategies to make information available:

1 Cooperative planning of courses and tasks
2 Moderation of work, leading to course evaluation and review
3 Systematic collection and collation of data
4 Library and abstract/review service
5 In-service training seminars

I have already outlined a model of a course evaluation and review process and how it can be used to make information more widely available. This model obviously depends on cooperative curriculum planning within a department/faculty, where information, ideas and experience are shared.

Systematic use of data

Other information should be routinely and systematically made available, for example, attendance figures, option uptake and achievement (including analyses by sex), and homework records. Much of this information can be collected quite simply, for example:

1 Where the tutor-set is the teaching group for most lessons, a daily attendance or record sheet can be carried round by a member of the tutor-set. Information on attendance, work, patterns of behaviour, homework, can be filled in by subject teachers and reaches tutors and pastoral heads daily

2 A simple weekly report by the pastoral head to senior management on attendance, tutor-sets or curriculum areas causing concern, referrals of students, etc

3 A pastoral year head is in a very good position to collect and collate data as students pass through the school. Much of the information would automatically be available in a school that was concerned to monitor children's work and performance. Such data might include longitudinal attendance studies, option choice figures, final examination performance (analysed by ability, sex and subject departments), longitudinal attainment studies. The last studies are only really useful if there is a whole-school policy about the awarding of *moderated* attainment grades or scores. The year head is the only person with that broad horizontal perspective of the school which allows some insight into the children's experience of learning and their performance across the curriculum. (The use of computer-assisted administration in schools should aid year heads in their collation and analysis of data.)

This kind of information allows staff to react speedily to specific problems, but it also facilitates effective line-management and gives a useful overview to management.

Writing a discussion document: the story so far

The argument I have put forward so far has sought to place the discussion document within a definite context. Discussion documents are most effective:
1 When there is a clear decision-making process established
2 When consultation involves the whole school and its communities
3 When issues arise from a planned evaluation and review process
4 When the school is organized to collect and disseminate information so that staff (in particular) are well informed.

It might be helpful at this stage to refer back to the examples listed on pages 8 and 9, and for each example to think about or discuss:
1 Who would make the decision
2 Who would be consulted
3 How the issues might have arisen from the evaluation-review process
4 What routinely collected information on the issue might be available.

However effective the continuous process of evaluation and information dissemination is within a school, there is a clear need for specific documents on definite issues, such as those referred to on pages 8 and 9. The flow diagram in Figure 1.4 summarizes the stages in putting the document together.

Identifying the issue (see Figure 1.4)

This has already been discussed earlier in the chapter (see pages 10–12). I have also indicated that a school should have a clear decision-making process which should make it easy to identify the writer and audience, and the exact nature and purpose of a particular document (for decision, for discussion, etc.). The purpose and the audience should be the major influence on the whole process of producing the document.

Gathering information (see Figure 1.4)

Information may be collected from three kinds of source:
1 Data and observation from within the school (see page 16)
2 Evidence from members of the school's communities (page 17)
3 Outside advice, experience and expertise (page 17).

However the information is collected, there are some *basic guidelines* that should be followed:
1 Be clear about how much information you need

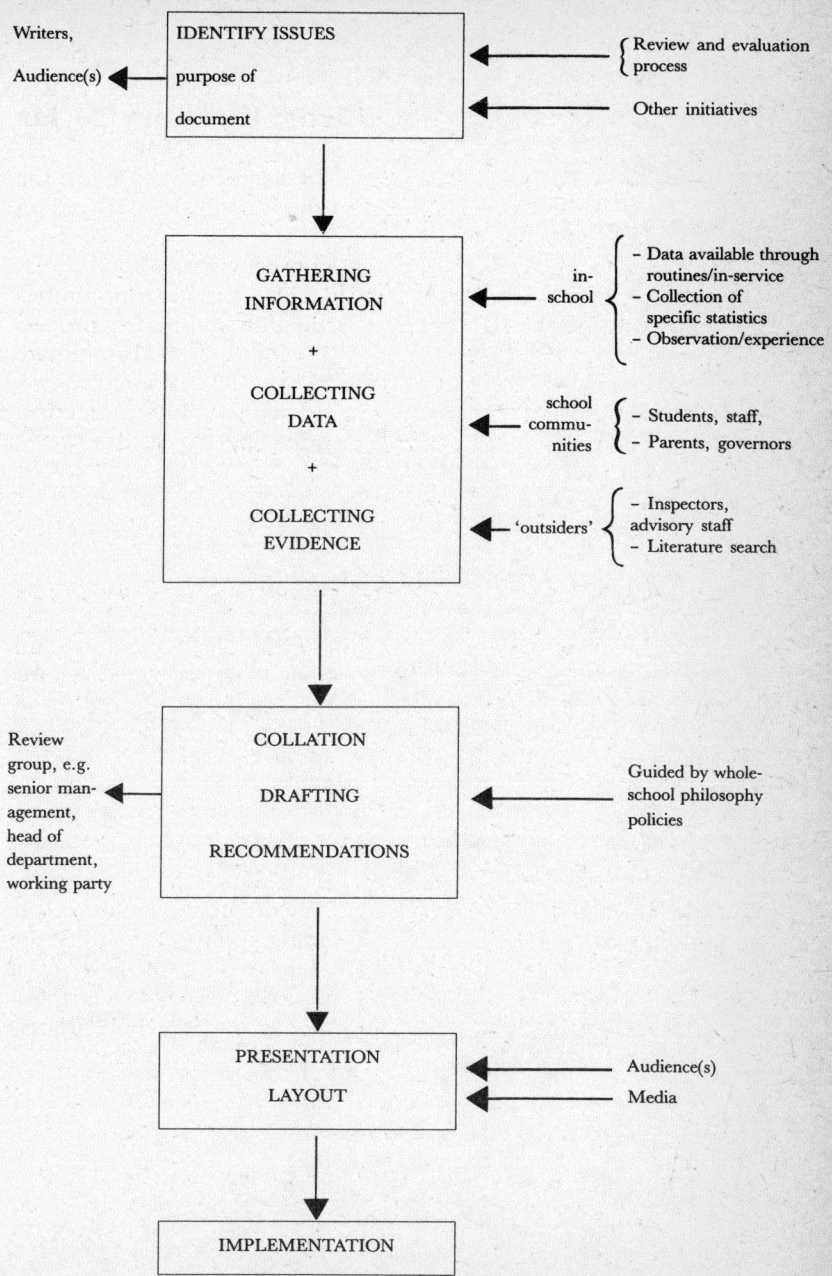

Figure 1.4   Flow diagram – putting the document together

2 Be clear about how much information you are prepared to collect
  – you are not collecting statistics for a major thesis or carrying out
  a controlled educational experiment
3 Be clear about the purpose of collecting information
4 Use information you already have, or can lay your hands on easily
5 Use other people's information and experience if they are relevant
  to your school.

In-school information
I have already illustrated how a school can be organized to make
available and to collect some of the information that often lies hidden
and unused. In addition to this kind of information, the writer may
decide to collate available information in a new format, or to collect
further data. For example, a working group reviewing the fourth-
year option scheme in a mixed school (one of the examples on page
9) would want to use school data already available on sexual differentiation in subject choice. In addition, it might want to use any
moderated achievement grades of the students in the third-year, to
analyse choice by attainment. The group might want to generate
new data by presenting students with an alternative way of grouping
options and asking them to make a new choice of subjects.

In the 1960s it seemed that educational research was only worthwhile if it involved statistics, figures, percentages, 'before' and
'after' attitude and performance tests, and chi-squared probability
tests. However, most in-school information can be collected from
observation (and without using a stopwatch!). An observer from a
working group on language can visit a range of classes over a term
and collect useful and significant evidence about the amount of
group discussion work; or on the modes of language used in set
tasks; or on the kinds of questioning techniques used by teachers,
etc. Random collections of students' work can give very useful
information on the marking policy (or lack of it) in a department; the
type and frequency of homework set; attitude to expressive
language. Teachers can act as researchers in their own classroom by
deliberately evaluating one aspect of their teaching, or their
students' learning, lesson by lesson. A subject department would use
this technique to help it to evaluate a new course unit, or a new
approach to teaching. The climate and philosophy of a school will
determine how successful this kind of observation is as a means of
collecting information. If the school encourages collaborative
planning of learning and the role of teacher as researcher, then it is
likely that teachers will regularly be in each other's classrooms and
swapping examples of children's work. (Routine cross-moderation
will also encourage these activities.) Co-observation agreements are
an effective non-threatening way into each other's rooms. For
example, teacher A invites teacher B into his/her class but only asks
for observation and comment on one particular aspect of his/her

teaching or classroom activity; then teacher B reciprocates choosing his/her own particular aspect.

Using the school's communities

Valuable information can be obtained directly from members of the school communities by interviewing. Referring again to one of the examples on page 9 – the reception of the new intake into a secondary school – the most important information here will be gained by talking directly to the children involved, both individually and in groups. Although the agenda for such interviews needs some broad agreement, the interviews should not be too structured, otherwise the researcher risks the danger of prejudging the issues and possibly missing vital information.

The collection of evidence need not necessarily consume a vast amount of teachers' time. In the example mentioned above, fifth- and sixth-year students could conduct some interviews, and help in drawing up possible agendas for the interviews, as a 'real' learning experience in their upper school courses. (The advantage of giving upper-school students real tasks related to their community hardly needs stating.) First-year students might interview fourth-year primary pupils about their impending transfer. Many parents would willingly help in providing information on this issue. This would have two added bonuses of getting parents involved in the secondary school, and giving the school the opportunity to explain some of its aims related to the induction of new pupils.

The use of governors as collectors of evidence for a working party or for a department has the advantage of educating governors about the school's educational aims at the same time as using them as a means of communication with the communities outside the school. More obvious examples of school issues where governors might contribute to the collection of information for a discussion document are: careers and work experience; courses involving direct community studies; contact with ethnic communities; links with colleges and other schools.

Using outside expertise

The writers of a discussion document only have recent first-hand experience of their own school, along with impressions of other schools from visits or from visiting speakers. The inspectorate and advisory teachers of the education authority have a broad range of experience of good practice in many schools. They are most likely to be able to provide support, advice and recommendations on a *subject specific* basis rather than on a whole-school or cross-curriculum concern. (It is regrettable that the local authority advisory service is still based mainly on subject expertise, when schools are increasingly concerned with the process of learning and with those things that are shared across the curriculum.) However, they can make major contributions to discussion documents by suggesting alternatives that have been tried in other schools; they can bring to the debate a wealth of knowledge and opinions from courses and in-service training; they can save departments from the task of 'reinventing the wheel'. What they generally do not possess is a good idea of the total context into which their recommendations will fit. For that reason, their evidence needs careful evaluation by members of staff.

A literature search can also provide experience from outside the school. A good in-service training programme which involves the librarian or library service is essential to keep staff up to date with educational concerns. However, when a specific issue is raised, it is helpful to collect together some of the current thinking and practice from other schools. For school discussion documents, a thorough literature search is not appropriate, unless the writer has a year's secondment! Where there is a school librarian, he or she should be asked to undertake the literature search.

The authority's education library will probably subscribe to the *British Education Index* (published quarterly with details of journal articles), the *British National Bibliography* (published weekly with listings of all books in Dewey Number order) or the *Current Index to Journals in Education*. Most schools will find even more useful one of the data bases which act as specialist sources on curriculum-related topics, including papers and publications not recorded elsewhere – for example, the Schools Council (now School Curriculum Development Committee) data base CRIS (Curriculum and Resource Information Service) which can readily produce a personalized list of references covering a specific topic; and the data base of the Centre for the Study of Comprehensive Schools based at the University of York, which will also produce a personalized list, including publications of subscribing schools.

Most discussion documents will be more informative and instructive if they contain that wider perspective of *tried* experience in other schools. An efficient literature search by a librarian or by using one of the databases can identify the articles and practices that are really relevant. Schools that do not use these facilities are being short-sighted, if not conceited; no one institution has the monopoly on good practice.

Collation and drafting (see Figure 1.4)

Although a good school encourages 'research, review and evaluation', its staff are classroom teachers, tutors and administrators; they have limited time to sit on committees to re-draft discussion documents; they have limited time to read and discuss documents. This indicates that the first draft should need the minimum number of changes and it should be as brief as possible.

The time taken to collate all the data and draft the discussion document obviously depends on the scale of the research and the importance of the topic. A major curriculum review working party might meet and research for one or two years, collecting evidence from different sources, reporting to itself as a committee and producing minutes, giving interim reports to staff meetings, and producing a final report from the whole working party based on its own minutes and interim reports. A head of year might wish to produce a report based on the year team's experience and their collected information on homework set for the year group. A head of department might produce a paper on a proposed new lower-school syllabus.

Is there any advice about the collation of evidence and information and the drafting of the paper that is common to all types of school discussion document? The following guidelines apply to most discussion documents.

Who drafts the paper?

One or two people should write the 'final draft'. If the draft is the responsibility of one person, he/she should show relevant sections to others who have collected evidence, and get at least one other person to proofread and criticize the draft. One person on their own is likely to allow weak argument to go unchallenged, to miss accidental errors, or to show unintentional (or deliberate) bias. Such weaknesses in a document are more likely to be identified and removed if another person is commissioned to read it for that particular purpose. If a poor draft gets submitted to a meeting, it may either go through unchallenged (because of pressure of business) or occupy too much time and cause too much argument.

House style

If the school has a house style for its documents – use it. Staff will be familiar with the style and will find key sections speedily. A house style that numbers sections, paragraphs and sentences clearly ('civil service style') has the great advantage that specific points can be readily identified.

Introduction

Write a brief statement of the exact purpose and outline content of the document. For example:

> This document describes the current arrangements for the induction of primary-school pupils into North End Secondary School. It has collected evidence from pupils, teachers at Little-folk Primary School, first-year tutors and teachers, parents and the head of year at South Side Secondary School. It makes several suggestions for improving the induction that should make the process of secondary transfer easier for pupils and parents.

Method

This section is often omitted, but readers do need to know how the document came into existence. There is more than a suspicion among staff at times that some documents should be prefaced by – 'After I left school, I went along to the Mouse and Trap, had a few beers and a chat with Fred, and came up with this brilliant scheme.'

If information and statistics are used as evidence, it is important to know, for example, how many classes were observed, and over what time span, how many parents were interviewed, how many homework diaries looked through, whose ideas are quoted, etc. However, do not go into full blow-by-blow details – you are not writing a thesis or a diary.

Evidence or information

Produce a summary of your information – there is no need to write all the detail; the evidence is there if anyone wants to see it. For example, if your document is on fourth-year option schemes, produce summaries of your own school's scheme, schemes from other schools, hypothetical schemes (from texts, for instance). Produce a summary table of 'pros' and 'cons' of the schemes based on interviews with parents, students, teachers, employers, etc. If you have researched the setting of homeworks, give summary statistics – 'Only 40 per cent of timetabled homeworks for the second year were set.' 'Ninety per cent of homeworks did not require the use of any textbook.' Do not make claims that are not substantiated by your evidence. Before you write 'Exclusive: Big Swing of Girls to Design Technology Options!', get someone with a statistics background to check that your claim is valid.

Conclusions

This section sums up all the information and evidence, reflects it back to the original purpose, and leads directly into the recommendations. This part of the draft needs very careful scrutiny. The conclusions must relate to the original purpose of the document, and they must be accurate in the light of the evidence collected. Conclusions may be definite (for example, 'It is evident that the school's homework policy is not being followed and no one is taking on the responsibility for monitoring homework'); or tentative (for example, 'There appear to be certain advantages and disadvantages in drawing up a common marking scheme for all subjects').

Recommendations

As with the conclusions, this section should definitely not be the work of only one person. Its final drafting should involve the staff, and outsiders, who will be primarily responsible for carrying out the implementations if they are agreed to. The recommendations need listing and numbering (and ordering in priority – at least in thought, if not in print). Where action is recommended, the draft should also recommend where the responsibility for action lies, and indicate a time-scale for action. The draft should be finally agreed by the relevant group or person (for example, senior management team, head of year, working party, etc.) before being produced in final form.

Presentation and layout

A very good case presented in a discussion document can be lost because of poor layout and presentation. If you publish an important document to staff in the second week of December, in your own error-ridden single-spaced typing, and with no meeting to launch it, you can expect it to elicit as much enthusiasm as an invitation to the school jumble sale. Generally, teachers are not renowned for their layout and presentation skills, so if there is an expert in school – for example a media resources officer – use him/her. It is *not* a misuse of his/her time and expertise. If you are convinced that your research, the document and its recommendations are truly important, then you should ensure they get serious consideration.

If the layout of the document becomes your responsibility, then the following guidelines should be observed:

1 It should be easy to read – with good spacing, clear indication of separate sections, etc.
2 It should be as short as possible
3 It should avoid unnecessary jargon words
4 Recommendations should be clearly highlighted – on a separate page and/or underlined and/or boxed
5 For lazy readers, there should be a summary of the main points of the document
6 Cartoons and graphics make points very effectively.

Most documents sink without trace unless they are presented to a meeting (staff meeting, department meeting, pastoral team meeting, etc.). The launching of a discussion document is an important event – it should not be taken lightly. Many documents have taken tens of 'person-hours' to write, yet their presentation is given only a few minutes' thought. The following points should be considered when a document is being presented to a meeting:

1 The document should be distributed in advance of the meeting, with clear indications in the document as to when it is to be discussed, how decisions are to be made and implemented, etc.
2 Audiovisual aids should be used during the presentation, especially overhead transparencies for emphasis of key points
3 Key facts, important evidence, conclusions and recommendations may be read out verbatim as not all the staff will have read the document.

Implementation

'There's many a slip 'twixt cup and lip' – and to write a penultimate section on discussion documents and their presentation followed by a bold heading, 'Implementation' seems to make assumptions about the making of decisions. A key management skill is to ensure a receptive audience. A great deal of time and thought and research goes into discussion documents and they need serious consideration. Their recommendations have a sound foundation; they represent the collective wisdom on an issue. The person in charge of the presentation of a document should spend time talking through its main points with some of the key people who will be at the meeting to discuss it and who will have to manage the implementation of its recommendations. Their understanding of the document and its recommendations is vital if they are to give it their full support.

The other reason for including this short section on implementation lies with the authors's own experience of meetings where everyone has agreed on the excellence of an idea and everyone has left the meeting feeling more than satisfied with the decisions that appear to have been made, and yet months later nothing has happened. The recommendations in a document should include proposals as to whose responsibility it is to carry out and oversee implementation, a timetable for implementation and review, and suggestions as to appropriate means of evaluation. These proposals also need discussing and finalizing at the decision-making meeting.

References

For publications concerned with the teacher as classroom researcher, there are many good examples available from CARN (Classroom Action Research Network) and the Ford Teaching Project, published by the Centre for Applied Research in Education (University of East Anglia) and the Cambridge Institute of Education.

HARGREAVES, D. (1982) *The Challenge for the Comprehensive School.* Routledge & Kegan Paul.

2   Arranging and Chairing Meetings

Lesley Bulman

Even in a small primary school or a small secondary department, much of the school management will centre round fairly formal meetings. The close informal before-school and breaktime coffee talk has great importance, of course, but it is no substitute for the teachers convening as a 'meeting'. The chairing of the variety of meetings that school management requires is a daunting challenge, different in a number of ways from meetings in other contexts. To be able to chair a meeting effectively is a key skill for school management.

MM

Most teachers spend one or more of their evenings after school at meetings. If the meetings are useful then they become extremely valuable as a method of in-service training as well as for planning. If they are not felt to be productive or interesting then teachers rightly see them as an unnecessary encroachment on their free time that could be more profitably spent. Whether meetings are valued as useful or resented as useless is largely in the control of the person chairing those meetings.

Many different meetings take place in a school – ranging from the fairly informal working party where the brief is straightforward, through departmental and pastoral team meetings, to school-wide meetings of academic and pastoral heads, up to the full formal staff meeting. Although all these meetings will have different items for discussion and different members, the skills needed to chair them are much the same.

Meetings can have many different functions, and these will to some extent determine the style of chairing required. In most school meetings, apart from working parties with a narrow focus on a particular problem, there will be a variety of functions dictated by the different items on the agenda. Meetings are normally required to define, approve or promote school policies, to decide on various lines of action, to explore the feelings of members, and to transfer information. Any school that values consultation will have long, detailed and controversial meetings to define new policies and to take decisions, and this will involve meetings at all levels within the school. Such meetings will be both difficult and rewarding to chair.

Because meetings take place in teachers' free time it is important that their frequency is kept to a minimum. There are two ways in which a chairperson can limit the number of meetings teachers have to attend: by ensuring that meetings are only held for discussions when this is appropriate, and also that only those people whose views are essential *have* to attend them.

Within a department, year, or school there will be a huge exchange of information and views. For the most part, this can be done by using letters, notices and memos. Staff will not need to be told in a meeting how to read a timetable, how to write a piece for the school brochure, or what items to include in a report – all this can be written down. (Clearly if there is confusion, or if new staff are involved, they may need individual explanation, but not in front of ten or so peers.) A meeting does become essential when the information is very dense and new, as in a new curriculum analysis or in a new method of recording examination results, or when the information is really promulgation of a new policy. However, it is surprising how many meetings I have attended where the basic format is the giving of information that should have been written down, and even more amazingly *has* been written down and is now being read out!

Meetings to discuss policy or to arrive at collective decisions are essential (providing there is still room for manoeuvre and the exercise is not sham-democracy). Meetings can make people feel more involved and responsible for their institution, help develop their educational background and train people for promotion, as well as radically increasing the school's access to expertise in a staff.

Not everyone needs to or should attend every meeting on everything. Even the most ardent democrats have not the time or energy to do this, and also taking decisions in a large meeting is very difficult. If real consultation is to take place, it is best to arrange meetings as part of a cycle with limited membership needing to attend the different meetings. For example, the following could be a cycle for school meetings for a half term:

Week	Monday	Tuesday	Wednesday	Thursday
1	Head and deputy		Departments	
2	Head and deputy	Head of department	Years	
3	Head and deputy	Head of year	Departments	
4	Head and deputy		Years	Staff
5	Head and deputy	Head of year	Departments	
6	Head and deputy	Head of department	Years	

Within a department meetings could follow this cycle:

Week	
1	
2	All staff
3	
4	Heads of subject and head of department
5	
6	Subject teachers

As each individual teacher is only a member of a few of these meetings the individual burden does not become too onerous, and there still remains plenty of evenings for clubs, detentions, and being with pupils. An extended cycle also allows time for individuals to talk to one another between meetings. Representatives of departments and years will have had the time to collect real feedback.

It is undoubtedly helpful for all staff if meeting dates are put into the school calendar in June for September. This allows staff to plan their after-school activities and will certainly improve their ability to attend. Meetings that are advising on decisions affecting the whole school (such as head of department meetings) should be open to all staff as observers. If the cycle is well known in advance, teachers who want to become involved have a chance to be so.

Finally, when planning meetings, it is as well to give a fixed finishing time and to stick to this. Teachers will need to know this in order to plan their lives and it is not fair to extend meetings arbitrarily when many may have to leave and feel disenfranchised as a result.

Agendas

Apart from very informal meetings of working parties where work is fairly continuous, all meetings should have agendas circulated in advance. Agendas are very brief simple documents, outlining the major items to be discussed during the meeting. They almost invariably follow this pattern:

Title of meeting
Date   Time   Place

Agenda
1.   Apologies for absence
2.   Minutes of the last meeting
3.   Matters arising
4. ⎫
.   ⎬ Items to be discussed
. ⎭

x   Any other business

End of meeting time

Although this may seem a little formal for colleagues in schools, it is an extremely useful preliminary to a meeting. Items (2) and (3) allow for some discussions on follow up to the last meeting which can be rewarding for those who were present and demonstrate that their efforts and decisions have been noted or acted on. 'Any other business' allows members, as well as the chair, to propose items that are new or urgent.

When arranging items to be discussed, they can either be put in order of priority, as time invariably runs out towards the end of a meeting, or if there are a few short items they can be put first so that they are properly dispatched before devoting the main body of the meeting to the one important issue. The order is important to establish on an agenda – as much precious time can be spent discussing the agenda as the items on it.

It is important not to have too many discussion items. It is not reasonable to expect people to discuss fruitfully at one meeting the new third-year curriculum, departmental allocation of resources, and a new assessment procedure. Even if they are put on an agenda in order to carry them on to another meeting, as a checklist, it is dispiriting to read and very frustrating if, for example, you have prepared a passionate appeal on finance and find yourself still discussing the position of Latin two meetings later. Agendas should be adhered to. If they are really taken as an outline of a meeting then staff will focus on the relevant items.

The final agenda for any meeting should be circulated in advance. It should be available a minimum of three days before the meeting so that representatives can consult and collect their thoughts and any data they require. Meetings that involve making decisions on matters that affect the whole school should be made public – either on a notice board or in a newsletter to all staff (including, of course, representatives of non-teaching staff).

Problems and discussions in a school year have a predictable cycle: Curriculum decisions have to be taken at the end of the autumn term, so curriculum discussion must take place early in that term, even though the following year seems very remote; the allocation of resources is usually in the summer term; discipline can be an acute problem in November. Major meetings on these and similar topics that are predictable and that will involve widespread discussion in the school should be planned with the school calendar for the year in the preceding June. Major agenda items for heads of department and house/year meetings can be planned around this cycle of decision deadlines published to staff at the beginning of the school year. This gives a framework for consultation so departmental and year meetings can also be planned to provide the advice and feedback to their representatives attending the major school meetings. Publication of major items also allows individual members of staff to make their views known independently of their departmental or pastoral channels and they can decide if they wish to attend the meetings as observers.

Although I plan the major items well in advance, I find it very helpful to have a folder labelled 'Head of department' where I slip in ideas and suggestions from other colleagues. It is from this reservoir of ideas that I draw up the final agenda for each meeting.

The environment

It is not sufficient as a chairperson to ensure that there are enough chairs for people to sit on at a meeting. It is important that some care is given as to how the room is arranged to meet the purpose of the meeting. Various patterns are possible.

Standard classroom

This is highly unsatisfactory for meetings that involve discussion. It is not easy always for the chairperson to see everyone and members of the meeting either will not be able to see each other talk or have to turn round most uncomfortably. Many school meetings do take place in classrooms but it is well worth a few moments time to rearrange the tables and chairs.

Circle of chairs

This is ideal for discussion and exchanging ideas – however, it is awkward if people have to use or refer to any papers. Working parties who want to establish a non-hierarchical group identity may find this seating appropriate.

Round a table

Probably this is the best format for most discussions. Each person is able to see the others, the table is there for papers, the chairperson is not too dominant but is clearly visible. It is important that the table should be big enough to accommodate all participants (it is easy for people to become 'bolshie' if relegated to a back row of chairs) and also that there are not too many people on each side or they will have difficulty seeing each other when they talk. If possible the room should not be too small. If there is any controversy it is much more likely to become aggravated in a small, hot, stuffy room.

Chairing the meeting

Procedures

Most school meetings, apart from working parties, will follow the normal rules of debate:

1 The chair controls the meeting
2 All remarks are addressed to the chair
3 Members do not interrupt each other
4 The aim is to reach a consensus
5 Votes are taken only if there is no consensus and when chair thinks
   it appropriate
6 A majority vote is accepted as the decision by all members
7 The outline of the meeting is determined by the agenda.

Apart from these simple, well established rules, the running of a
meeting is very much in the hands of their chairperson. It is not
necessary to have a working knowledge of Citrine's *The ABC of
chairmanship* as it might be in some political meetings.

Starting the meeting

Be there before anyone else arrives. Have the room arranged as you
want it and your papers laid out so there is easy access to any
documents you might need. Have paper and a pen ready and clear
sight of a clock or watch. Tea at the beginning of a meeting is a great
distracter. The meeting should start sufficiently long after school for
those who need tea to have time to down a quick cup, but providing
tea and biscuits at the beginning of a meeting will delay the start by
ten or fifteen minutes. It is important to emphasize a prompt start.
Many will complain, or leave, if your meeting goes on ten or fifteen
minutes longer than scheduled. Therefore a prompt start is vital.
Calling for apologies and asking if the minutes are correct is an easy
way to begin the meeting.

I always have a copy of the minutes starred or with notes for
matters arising so that I can quickly report on progress and action.
This should be brief and members wishing to re-enact the last
meeting (and to overturn decisions they did not like) should be
firmly hushed up. Any item that was left unresolved or requires
detailed and lengthy reports back should be on the agenda as an item
so that this section of the meeting should be quite quick.

Introducing items

I have found that for almost all major items on an agenda a
preliminary document is essential. It is possible to have meetings
where an item involves a hugely open-ended discussion and
members are expected to talk freely to arrive at a 'feeling' (for
example: 'Would we want to introduce setting in the fourth and fifth
years?'). However, I feel that often such meetings result in a
purposeless airing of private prejudices and leave people very
dissatisfied. Even with very open-ended questions I think it helps to
focus people's minds if they have had a document beforehand
outlining the situation with pros and cons. Imparting information in
a meeting is often an unworthy use of people's precious time. Again,

it is better to present the information as a document and to take queries and discuss its implications at the meeting itself. It is the really big issues in a school that are likely to be the most controversial and therefore the most difficult to chair. It is wise to have planned a very clear structure beforehand, and a discussion document readily provides this.

Proposals for changes of policy require a time to gestate as well as to be talked over. Therefore the following schedule, although time-consuming, provides a realistic timescale for making acceptable decisions:

Week	1	Issue of discussion document
	2	Meeting for preliminary discussion
	3, 4	Consultation period
	5	Meeting for report back and decision-taking.

Circulating documents beforehand means that the introduction of the topic to the meeting has to some extent been done. Having assumed that everyone has already read the document, it is unforgivable if the chairperson then goes through the document in detail point by point – or, even worse, reads it through. (This may seem self-evident but it is done and certainly takes up a lot of meeting time.) Sometimes it is useful to pick out one or two key sentences, sometimes to reiterate the circumstances that have led to the document, but after that the floor should be open for queries.

Asking for any queries or clarification of the document is a good opening. Many points will need amplification or explanation. It is a very open-ended way of initiating discussion, people feel free to inquire and express approval or disapproval of sections and the scene is set for later discussion. When the document is long and controversial, most of the preliminary discussion can be devoted to asking questions and exploring rather than taking sides. Representatives who will then have to explain the document to others are well informed and able to pass on accurately its meaning and intention. (This aspect of meetings provides one of the most useful means of in-service training in schools.)

Different types of document require different handling. Documents containing a lot of coded or difficult information (such as a curriculum analysis) will need a lot of explanation, but once that is done the document will have served its purpose in providing information. Some documents will require acceptance from the meeting in order to become policy; others will require the meeting to choose between alternatives.

With policy documents, once the query stage is over it is important that the meeting discusses the main principles behind the document. If the main principle is accepted then the document can be improved and refined by moving through it clause by clause. In the case of a highly controversial document often the basic premise is not fully accepted and then it is a case of whittling away clause by clause so that agreement is reached on some items. This is not as dispiriting to a chairperson (who presumably wants the document to become policy) as it sounds. Although the policy as a totality may not have been passed, much that is desirable will have been accepted, and many ideas have been sown that may well come to fruition later.

When meetings have to decide on one or other of various proposals the item can be introduced either by calling for questions on a prepared document or by calling on the various proposers of the alternatives to speak briefly or by the chairperson quickly going through the implications of the various alternatives. If members of the meeting have a very strong interest in one proposal rather than another then they should be called upon to speak. If one member of the meeting has a strong point of view but is too shy to speak or has low status within the group, then he/she should be specifically invited to comment and the point of view restated clearly by the chairperson.

After this initial setting of the scene it is important to talk about the elimination of proposals and the criteria that can be used for such elimination. When choosing, it is much simpler to eliminate proposals that do not match all or most of the criteria than it is to select the best. In a very difficult meeting on the fourth- and fifth-year curriculum and period allocation where there were nine proposals on the table, two were simply eliminated at this stage by their proposers who could see other alternatives that matched the criteria better than their own.

When there are several possible solutions it is vital for the chairperson to keep refocusing on the criteria and also that he/she looks for the next 'gate' proposal. Some proposals, if accepted, mean that all the other proposals would automatically be eliminated and therefore such proposals must be taken first. For example, again from the fourth- and fifth-year curriculum discussion, there was one proposal for a compulsory curriculum for all pupils except for one option block. As all the other proposals involved three or more option blocks, if this proposal had been accepted, then the discussion on the other eight alternatives would have ended. (It was not accepted.) It is the role of the chairperson to spot this mutual exclusivity and to focus on these proposals in turn.

In my own experience the chairperson of a school meeting is rarely truly neutral. You have drawn up the agenda according to your own or the school's priorities. There are proposals and priorities that you feel very committed to or are expected to promote. Proposals and policies have been thoughtfully prepared – there is a great desire for the favoured policy, etc., to be passed by the meeting, but sometimes meetings will not be persuaded. Part of your planning as a chairperson is to put your preferred case clearly and as persuasively as possible – but it is also important to know what alternatives would be acceptable and not to battle on for your own pet solution. Often the collective thoughts of other colleagues improve solutions radically and this should be publicly welcomed. Even if your more radical proposals are rejected it may be that some aspects can be accepted with a feeling on the part of the chairperson that everyone involved has become a little more informed as a result of the discussion. It can be hard not to become too heavily identified, involved, even angry and disappointed, but it is important to retain humour and stoicism. I remember reeling out of a very difficult meeting where I felt that members had been very hostile, negative and reactionary, but during the intervening weeks before our final discussions on the matter I realized that the meeting had stimulated the most creative solution to our problem and that not only the people who had been at that meeting but other members of staff were really thinking very deeply. The next meeting was extremely exciting indeed with heads of departments and many observers really debating in an informed caring way that was a challenge and a pleasure to chair!

Dealing with the 'difficult'

These are some of the problems a chairperson will have to deal with:

The dominant person: 'As *I* was saying, *I* think the *only* solution is *my* solution. *I* know about . . . '

The long-winded person: 'It's sort of like this really . . . ' etc. (5 minutes); 'and also sort of like this . . . ' etc. (5 minutes); 'and in some ways sort of like this . . . ' etc. (5 minutes).

The quiet, inhibited person: 'Umm . . . I'm not sure, I'm no good at this.'

The angry, bitter person: 'You've always had it in for my tutor group! You don't like me!'

The territorial person: 'My department wants *more*.'

The warhorse: 'Well, as I keep saying, it all comes down to the fact that my department hasn't enough money.'

The action replay – and replay: 'I think we should look again at the decision taken at last month's meeting.'

Decisions are devisive and nasty: 'Do we have to decide now?'

The democrat: 'We can't decide because we need more time/data to discuss/consult.'

Taking a class lesson and chairing meetings are remarkably similar activities and most advice for dealing with difficult members would apply equally happily to both!

It is important to be well prepared mentally and emotionally, especially before controversial meetings. It is useful, if possible, to set aside half an hour immediately before the meeting begins to go through the papers again, draw up points one wishes to make on the previous minutes or on the documents, note 'any other business' that must be dealt with, and think oneself into the agenda. During the days beforehand I will have put into my meeting folder any data or ammunition that I think I might need and during the half hour before the meeting I try to run through in my mind any other possible questions or information that might be required and put it in the folder. Ten minutes before the meeting begins arrange the room, lay out your papers in order and sit down and try to be relaxed and confident.

Dealing with different members of a meeting requires a teacher's mixture of firmness, fairness, knowledge of personalities, and above all a sense of humour. Someone is bound to become aggressive or antagonistic towards the chair during a meeting, and a little joke, a sense that you have things firmly in perspective and are not going to be riled, angry or upset is very important indeed.

Time is a great ally. Meetings will always tend to overrun so references to time can be called on to shorten a too-lengthy diatribe, curb the irrelevant or silence the over-dominant without antagonizing the meeting. If you are to be firm about others' contributions then it is only fair to control your own. It can be tempting to expound or lecture as no one has the power to stop the chair, but it is fatal.

Calling on members to speak is fairly and easily done if you jot down their names in order and cross them off as they are called. If you give a little nod to indicate they have been seen, it saves some wearying hand-waving. When a lot of people wish to speak it is useful to say aloud: 'Ann, Saleh, Andreas', so that they know their order.

Sometimes there will be antagonism and even anger shown between two protagonists. Some of these antagonisms are easily predicted; if one department is to gain at the expense of another and feelings are running high then some possibly angry exchanges are likely. In these circumstances vigilance is essential to gauge the emotional atmosphere. It is also helpful if both sides are allowed to state their positions openly and then for the chair to thank them and perhaps, if necessary, de-emotionalize the situation by summarizing the basis of each person's position. The protagonists should not be allowed to dominate the meeting, and a call for other comments after the summary by the chair helps to keep the discussion open. Under these circumstances the chair must demonstrate impartiality or there will be very great resentment. Meetings can be very useful under these circumstances in finding acceptable compromises or producing lateral thoughts that solve the problem (if one is lucky).

Keeping order can be quite difficult. Just as in class, a look or a glance can quieten down the chatterboxes. Firmness may be slightly resented at the time by the recipient but is valued by the meeting as a whole. Humorously or firmly sometimes people will have to be told that they have spoken for long enough, they are repeating points made, their ideas are quite unworkable, or totally off the point. Providing one is not rude or harsh one can even interrupt the flood of discourse with a 'Thank you, Bill, I'm glad you said that but . . . *time* is pressing', ' . . . I really don't think that's in our brief', ' . . . we've discussed this before, haven't we?', ' . . . wasn't that Joan's point?' (One caution – I know that I now have very fixed expectations of members of meetings I have chaired for a long time, and when some people begin to talk I reach for my termination sentence too quickly, and I have to pause to listen before preventing the expected monologue on the favourite subject that may sometimes not emerge.)

Throughout the meeting a chairperson must try not to dominate it with his/her own ideas. The chairing must be firm but fair and not antagonistic. Timing is the key to success, with contributions kept as short as possible while allowing people to express their ideas and feelings. People should feel that each member of the meeting has been offered a fair amount of time and that neither the chair nor the more vocal members have been allowed to dominate. The focus must be kept closely on the issues on the table and brief summaries provided by the chair at intervals so people know what is happening.

Drawing a discussion to a close

In a lengthy debate it is as well to signal quite a few minutes before you feel the discussion should end that time is drawing to a close. This makes the final contributions more pithy and gives members time to make their decisions. It is nice to do a quick verbal round up of all those who wish to speak, warning them that there is only five or so minutes left and will they please be brief. It is not a good idea to leave people with contributions unsaid.

The chair should attempt a summary of the discussion only if it has been quite simple and clear cut – otherwise the whole meeting will have to be re-run which is too time-consuming. If the discussion has been very wide ranging then it is better to refocus only on the original proposals. Finally, there is the assessment of the outcome of the meeting. This might be an amended document, a 'feeling of the meeting', or a vote on the proposals. Any outcome should be very clearly recorded in the minutes. Once this has happened then the discussion must be declared closed.

After the meeting

Minutes

After the meeting there are the minutes to be written. This, in my opinion, should be done by the chairperson. It is a useful exercise in reassessing the meeting, in reappraising its outcomes, and also as a method of moulding opinion. Emphasis on positive aspects can make useful a meeting that may have been very diffuse. If you are to chair a meeting sensitively though, it is important to be free to do only that and to leave taking notes for the minutes to someone else.

The taking of notes in a meeting is a chore often got round by rotating the task among members. This is not very satisfactory. People may be too involved in the discussion to be adequate note-takers or frustrated at not being able to participate in the discussion because they are taking notes. Furthermore, other people's notes are sometimes hard to read, writing up minutes is laborious, and if you have to translate different people's personal shorthand after each meeting the burden may become so great that the minutes get postponed even longer than your natural reluctance would determine. A deputy could take on this duty, or you could inveigle a more junior, but interested, member of staff to do this. In one school, a junior member of staff with a scale point minutes all the major cycle of meetings.

As a chairperson it is important to signal to the note-taker if you want something taken down most particularly. Verbal or facial hints are enough usually but when you, as chair, want the whole meeting to know that a summary or decision has been taken on board, it reassures the meeting if you actually say 'I would like this to be minuted' before repeating the comment or decision. (Clearly it is better to signal beforehand that something is to be minuted rather than say afterwards 'Can you minute that please?')

It is also useful if the note-taker jots down who is speaking beside comments raised in the meeting, and this is recorded in the minutes. For instance, when a very controversial period allocation was discussed, one dissenting head of department who had had his allocation reduced said that I had 'saved his bacon' with his staff as they had read in the minutes of his vocal oppositon. (It would not be fair, of course, to use minutes to diminish a colleague's reputation.)

There is a very natural tendency to postpone the writing of minutes. This is understandable but it is better for yourself and others if the minutes are written while the meeting is fresh in your mind – and well before the next meeting is due. Often the minutes will be needed by the head or deputies for making decisions or for members of staff to help consultation. The minutes should be made available in the same way as the agendas, with a copy on the notice board for all staff. It is politic to keep the notes taken during the meeting until the next meeting. After 'matters arising' has passed without adverse comment on the minutes then these notes can be thrown away. It is essential to keep a file of all agendas and minutes of meetings with any other documentation that was used at the meeting.

Follow-up

However stimulating a meeting, people will become quite resentful if nothing appears to happen as a result. Although it is tempting to put off doing the things you have promised, it has an extremely positive effect if notes, etc., are written the following day so that everyone knows that words are being put into action.

Some follow-up can be quite disagreeable. Meetings often call upon the head or deputies to do something that they will not or cannot do. As a head of department I always send copies of the minutes automatically to the head and the deputy in charge of the curriculum, with particular points they should notice marked clearly. If items are likely to cause great anger or irritation or need an explanation, then it is wise, if a bit daunting, to deliver the minutes in person. Reports of such a meeting and comments on the minutes will need to be brought up under 'matters arising' in the next meeting. It is not a good idea to delay delivering the minutes as bad news travels very quickly in a school.

As a chairperson I always make my own notes during a meeting of things that I must do and then go through the notes of the meeting immediately afterwards and draw up a list. I try to ensure that I do all the items on the list as quickly as possible and certainly to have done something by the next meeting. Questions on matters arising when all the chair can do is apologise for inaction can be very embarrassing indeed for the chair and dispiriting for the members of the meeting.

Running a successful meeting brings the same rewards as taking a good lesson. As with a good lesson knowledge and skilful handling of people in a meeting is not sufficient: time has to be spent on preparation and on follow-up. It is worth spending the time – not only will *you* enjoy the meeting more but so will all the other people who have given up their time to attend.

3 Appointment of Teachers

George Phipson

A wide range of staff take a part in the appointment of teachers, yet there is a tendency to presume it is 'all done by the head'. In secondary schools, middle-management responsibility holders are virtually always involved, in primary schools sometimes. Appointments, whether external or internal, scale 1 or senior, are crucial, and yet people get very little practice or opportunity to consider the technicalities or skills.

MM

The appointment of teachers to schools has traditionally seemed to be a subject of interest only to those directly involved in the process at the time, or as the butt of some staffroom joke about the inept questioning of a member of the interviewing panel. Little did we realize that the tensions of the candidates and the pressures on those appointing were the stuff of popular television until *Kingswood* held the nation in suspense as its head, Brian Tyler, fought to make the right appointment to his deputy headship. But in a profession which above all else depends for success on the quality of its members and their ability to forge good working relations between themselves, and between them and their pupils, then the skills needed to make sound appointments are paramount. The aims and philosophies of different institutions will be reflected in the qualities they seek in candidates and equally those same qualities will only be used to full effect in the right post. The process of selection should be two-sided offering the greatest possible opportunities for the success of future relationships to be judged. That said, it would be foolish not to acknowledge that in schools the authority vested in governors and headteachers to make appointments is one of the most effective ways that they can influence the quality of the education their pupils receive. Since the promotion and subsequent career development of their staff is similarly dependent upon them it is a responsibility which carries great power.

Timing

Turning to the practical management skills of the appointing process then, as with so much else in management, the ability to control, rather than be controlled by, time is crucial. The cycle begins at the moment when the head has a staffing position to fill which in mid-year probably means receiving notification of a resignation but when linked to planning the new academic year becomes a far more complex and uncertain matter. It goes without saying that the earlier a resignation is received the more helpful it is, yet the simplest study of the contractual resignation deadlines of full-time assistant teachers reveals obvious contraints:

> Resignation by 31 October for spring term start in new post
> Resignation by 28/29 February for summer term start in new post
> Resignation by 31 May for autumn term start in new post.

But from a point of view of a school receiving a resignation and wishing to appoint a successor to take over so that there is no discontinuity of teaching, these dates have to take account of the minimum period needed from the placing of advertisements to the confirmation of the appointment of the successful candidate. If, for example, this needed a minimum of a month, then a school will be vulnerable to staffing discontinuity if an existing member of staff resigns after September in the autumn term or January in the spring term. The summer term is the natural moment for promotion within the profession and the May 31st deadline takes on immense significance as timetables are being constructed for the following year. This is only partly mitigated by the fact that new entrants to the profession seeking their first post are not constrained by it. Thus it is already clear that an ability to streamline and speed up the appointing process is a valuable asset.

Staffing allocations

The great majority of decisions about staffing positions are inexorably linked to the annual cycle of local education authority resource planning. Many LEAs give schools three-year staffing forecasts based on projections of likely roll numbers and target staffing ratios. It is thus possible for a head to see the implications of current decisions in the light of the measures that will be required in the future to – all too often – reduce staff numbers. Much can be said about the curriculum and staffing consequences of falling rolls but within the context under discussion it must be emphasized that every decision to make an appointment will be the result of a very detailed and thorough analysis of future needs. Further because all teachers are increasingly aware of the instability caused by falling rolls, open discussion within the school is more likely to create an atmosphere in which the necessity of, say, redeployment from one area of the curriculum at the same time as external appointments are made to another area, is accepted.

As well as the internal stresses caused by falling rolls, appointments will also be affected by the global LEA position. It has become, regrettably, increasingly common for a head to have constraints imposed as to the field of candidates from which recruitment can be made. This so called 'ring fencing' is usually applied so as to limit all vacancies to those teachers already working for that LEA but can, for example, in the case of the reorganization of an area, limit the range of potential applicants even more severely. The appointing headteacher will only be fair to all concerned – candidates, school and ultimately pupils – if within the ring-fence the overriding principle remains that an offer is only made if and when the needs of the post are met.

The need to keep flexibility in adjusting staffing levels in schools has vastly increased the number of posts of a temporary nature now being advertised. Indeed, some LEAs are virtually insisting that all vacancies are advertised as temporary, with often disastrous effects on the range of candidates thus attracted to apply. There are clearly cases when the post is genuinely temporary in the light of curriculum/staffing plans for the following year, but on other occasions candidates report 'unofficial' assurances about long-term stability and then have to risk their careers becoming a form of musical chairs. In fairness to all concerned it should be made plain why the post is temporary – secondment of post holder, maternity leave, planned staffing contraction or whatever – with also a clear indication of the time-scale.

Posts of responsibility

If the post to be filled is to carry above-scale-1 responsibilities, then the decisions that surround it will involve the deployment of 'Burnham Points'. Each school is assessed, normally triannually, on the basis of the number of pupils in various age groups to establish a point score from which is derived its 'Group' – giving the level by which deputy head and headteacher salaries are calculated – and also its allowance of Burnham Points used in establishing posts above scale 1. A scale 2 post uses one Burnham Point, a scale 3 post uses two, scale 4 uses three, as does senior teacher. The resignation of a scale 3 post holder need not necessarily imply that a scale 3 vacancy will be advertised. Indeed, traditional school management was in the past very much associated with a headteacher's patronage in the deployment of such points. However, it is now not uncommon for there to be open discussion at a school's senior staff conference about the best allocation of available Burnham Points. Sadly, falling rolls has its impact on the number of such points and so on the promotion opportunities within the profession. The Burnham regulations provide for cushioning as a school moves down a group and for individual salary protection, but nonetheless as a scarce resource their deployment requires careful plannning often working towards a shadow structure based on the new lower number of points. Advertisements offering 'scale 2 or scale 3 for suitably qualified applicant' raise many questions and perhaps reflect more a reaction to external market forces than to internal job specification. Indeed, it has always seemed somewhat anomalous that in a profession pre-eminently concerned with people and interpersonal relations, posts of responsibility are all too often defined in terms of administrative tasks – 'scale 2 deputy head of department responsible for stock and examination entries'. Surely the prime responsibility in any post is for people – teams of teachers and groups of pupils – which leads us into job descriptions.

Job specifications

Before any job can be advertised, whether nationally or just internally, there must be clear agreement on the detailed job specification. In drawing this up it could be helpful to consider the role in four contexts: the pupils, other staff, administrative tasks, and the whole school. The balance and emphasis will vary between these four depending on the specific job, both as between scale 1 through to scale 4/senior teacher, and as between head of department, head of year, head of resources centre, and so on. Much behavioural research has highlighted the way interpersonal relationships depend on the perceived role in the mind of the individual, and though this perception is built on a clear job specification the interpretation will vary widely from individual to individual. Thus is a job description for a scale 4 head of house intended to ensure a uniformity of approach or to foster an individualistic house character and spirit? In so far as one can judge the collective quality of relationships within a school, then perhaps it is seen as the ethos – referred to in much research. Will a definition of aims and philosophies actually encompass the school's ethos?

As the task at this point is to examine the job specification within the whole cycle of making an appointment, then the need is to formulate satisfactory documentation that will allow an applicant a reasonable opportunity to sense the requirements of the job within the school. There will then be the further opportunity for short-listed candidates to visit the school and make their own judgements of the atmosphere and the role structure. Probably the best arrangement is to have a single document describing the school in general and then further details of the actual post.

The description of the school will need to include key facts and figures, status, size, age range, community/catchment area, site(s), buildings, staffing, resources, examination results. Within this context the aims and philosophies which underpin the educational arrangements within the school are followed by the resulting organization – curriculum, guidance, role/responsibility structure, and so on. Then there are details which will be of particular concern to applicants not familiar with the area or LEA – housing and commuting possibilities, schemes of assistance with removals and, perhaps above all else, an indication of how the school is placed with regard to falling rolls and possible reorganization plans.

The specific details of the post would be provided in an additional document giving the relevant background information about the department in which the vacancy lies, and listing the areas of responsibility. However, it may be that the school has a policy document outlining the responsibilities of, for example, heads of department or head of year, in which case this would be an obvious document to include.

Clearly the aim of sending out such information is to encourage application from teachers who are likely to be sympathetic with the aims of the school and who are prepared to take on the responsibilities outlined. However, the legal position as to what is included within a teacher's contract is complex and it would certainly be unwise for either the school or the applicant to view the job specification as a legal extension of the contract. It will certainly not cover all aspects of what is by 'custom and practice' a teacher's professional commitments, nor will much more than the 'status' of the job be ultimately protected in any reorganization. Perhaps the most important aspect of the documentation a school sends out is the impression it gives of the life and work of a school. A bald statement, as is not uncommon for deputy heads, that the precise responsibilities will depend on the abilities of the successful candidate, is an alternative approach to getting the working relationships right.

Before leaving the subject of job specification it seems relevant to consider the increasing need for a school to find within one person the ability to undertake two unrelated roles. Thus a school in which a head of house who was also a mathematician has resigned is faced by trying to find a mathematician – never an easy task – and also a head of house. This dilemma is often almost parodied in the classic 'Teacher of ———— required, ability to coach rugby an advantage'. In easier times one could bank on a sufficient movement of staff to go for the best 'head of house' at interview and adjust the subject teaching needs accordingly. The problem can be even more acute for senior teachers where very often leadership of a major department is linked to some senior school-wide responsibility. A recent advertisement for a senior teacher combined the responsibilities of head of English and of examining all departmental schemes of work for racial and sexual discrimination. Certainly a school may be fortunate in finding two such qualities within a single applicant, but the risk of not succeeding to do so on the first round may make the whole appointing process very protracted.

Drafting advertisements and the reply

Each LEA has an agreed procedure on advertising appointments and unfortunately this very often restricts the school. First, with speed often being of the essence, LEA procedures tend to draw out the deadlines; schools therefore need to be aware of when the form must be at the area office, or whatever. They also frequently limit the number of words that can be inserted; if this abbreviated insert appears as part of a County block advertisement it may be unnecessary to include details of closing dates and how the application should be made as these will form part of the block itself. However, one way or another certain minimum information should be included: subject/responsibilities/scale; school size/age range/type; method of application/further details/closing date. The law does not allow discriminatory copy in advertisements and normally schools should not anyway wish for it. Certain restrictions on applicants might apply in the case of residential education, or of church schools seeking 'reserved' teachers, or for physical education staff supervising changing rooms, for example. However, the scope of Genuine Occupational Qualifications giving exception to the Race and Sex Discrimination Acts is very limited and the LEA should certainly be consulted before so advertising. While on points of law, it may be as well to recall that under the Rehabilitation of Offenders Act, teachers applying for posts may be required to disclose spent convictions.

The ideal closing date is one which allows enough time for further details to be sent out as even the fullest advertisement must leave out a great deal. If schools really find the cost of postage an intolerable burden there is no reason why respondents should not telephone the school to ask for details. The further advantage of sending out details initially is that a county application form can also be sent. This ensures that applicants will include all the necessary details in a standard format. However, where applications by letter are invited these details are still needed.

Before leaving the subject of advertisements it is worth introducing an element of lateral thinking on the matter of where and when they appear. Traditionally they are circulated within the LEA in a county circular or whatever and then may be advertised nationally in *The Times Educational Supplement* and *The Teacher*. Some posts, particularly part-time or temporary ones, will only be placed in the local paper. There are obviously times of the year when the response to any advertisement will be very limited, such as Christmas, and these are best avoided. But there is also the possibility that potential applicants will miss such advertisements altogether. If a school is within easy rail/commuting distance of a town not covered by the local paper, private funds used to place an additional advertisement may pay off, or a card sent for display at a university department of education may be more publicly available than the junior common room copy of the *TES*. It is also wise to look at how the advertisement actually appears in print – remembering how a part-time vacancy in needlework appeared once in a local paper with a typographical error 'Headteacher required' rather than 'requires', thus resulting in much local rumour.

References and testimonials

Once applications have been received and sifted a long list will be drawn up and references sought. Most schools will have a standard *pro forma* letter for this and a stamped and addressed reply envelope should be enclosed. Some of these letters give a deadline for short-listing or request a speedy reply but this should be unnecessary as, certainly with a professional referee, the need for no undue delay should be well understood. Further it should come as no surprise to the referees in that the applicant should have secured their consent to act in that capacity before applying.

However, a note of caution must be entered at this point. The traditional difference between a testimonial and a reference was that a testimonial was an open document made available to the person of whom it was written, whereas a reference was a confidential document not seen by the person to whom it referred but sent direct to the person requesting it – the safeguards in the system being that an applicant named the referees. This distinction has now become somewhat eroded and confused.

First, testimonials as such have fallen into disuse partly on the grounds that their openness made them of little use as their comments were mild and superficial. But the correspondingly greater significance and power of confidential references has caused concern, especially as they are taken up from people not nominated by the applicant (in particular from the heads, whether nominated or not, as part of an LEA to LEA contact). Some authorities now insist that references must be open in that they must be shown to the teacher concerned. Further, the professional codes of the various teachers' unions underline the feeling that reports made by teachers on teachers should not be secret (see, for example, the NUT Professional Conduct Code (article b) with footnotes). If one adds to this the fact that it is not unheard of for a confidential reference to be returned to the applicant by mistake, then it becomes increasingly difficult to know the context in which such reports are written.

It is also instructive to examine what evidence a headteacher, say, will use in drawing up such a reference. On the basis that the views of the appropriate head of department and head of year will be sought, then the reference begins to take on the role of a catalyst for in-school evaluation; indeed, some schools have made an annually updated open reference the focus for a staff evaluation and development programme.

Returning to the request for a reference, the reply may well be general and not cover points specific to the actual post. Enclosing the full job description and asking for an indication of the suitability of the applicant is unlikely to help resolve this. The reference could be expected to have two main elements and interpretations of these must be up to the recipient.

One element is an assessment of professional qualities and achievements and may well cover the full spectrum with favourable or unfavourable comments in each area. If the areas covered seem selective but the comments generally favourable it seems reasonable to infer that the missing areas would have called for rather more contentious assessments. However, as reading between the lines is fairly generally practised, it is a warning to those writing references that they may do less than justice to a worthy candidate if they unintentionally fail to explicitly praise performance in a key area.

The other element is some indication of the level at which, overall, the candidate is recommended for the post or for promotion in general. Coded language is used to distinguish between 'recommend for consideration', 'recommend for interview', 'confidently recommend for the post', and so on. In fact of course the referee is not to know necessarily at what point in the whole process the reference will be used. It may be that only candidates called for interview are having their reference taken up thus making the first two comments superfluous while the last seems to pre-empt the need to interview at all.

Some headteachers clearly despair at having to decode references and instead send out a *pro forma* reference initially, thus ensuring an assessment of key areas and some unequivocal level of recommendation (see Figure 3.1).

It must also be said that, whether through pressure of time or despair at even profile referencing, heads do resort to the telephone on occasions. The practice is frowned upon by professional associations and invites hasty and less considered judgements. There is a clear distinction here between reading a reference over the telephone when deadlines are tight (and sending a confirmatory copy by post) and seeking off-the-record comments.

	Outstanding	Good	Average	Below average
Teaching ability				
Relationships with pupils				
General discipline				
Relationships with staff				
Leadership				
Administrative skills				
Soundness of judgement				
Ability to innovate				
Commitment				
Health and attendance				
Punctuality and presentation				

Would you recommend the applicant for a similar post at your school

(a) with confidence   (b) with reservation   (c) with hesitation

Figure 3.1   Example of a pro forma reference

Short-listing

The drawing up of a short list from among the applicants may be a pleasantly taxing task when the field is good or a sadly straight-forward matter when it is not. The LEA may lay down guidelines as to who must be involved depending on the scale of the post and would typically include the subject adviser or school inspector. The governors too may well wish to be involved through either the chairperson or staffing subcommittee. Short-listing is a very influential stage as it is then that the field is narrrowed towards candidates offering certain specific qualities – a commitment to mixed-ability teaching, a belief in a common curriculum or resource-based learning.

It would seem ill advised to draw up a short list without having consulted those most directly involved, such as the relevant head of department, though it would not be right to give wide circulation to information given in confidence. There is also a difficulty when there are internal candidates and those who might naturally be consulted are seen as having a vested interest. They may prefer to be seen as impartial to help achieve smooth acceptance of the eventual outcome.

Invitations to attend for interview will need to be sent out once the short list is complete and again a *pro forma* letter will speed up the process. A prompt note of acceptance of the invitation will also be required and it can be helpful to ask those who originally applied 'by letter' to complete an LEA form as this will give the interviewing panel a standard form of CV and may anyway be ultimately required of the successful candidate by the LEA. It will also be necessary to indicate clearly the time when candidates are expected to arrive and courteous to indicate the format of the day (or days) and include other domestic details such as train times, local street plan, etc.

The visit

Except for very senior posts LEAs seem unwilling to incur the additional expense of separating a visit to the school from the actual selection process/interview – though it should be said in passing that some headteachers will not even short-list until applicants have visited the school. The rationale for this certainly accords with popular experience that even a brief and superficial meeting can create a clear and lasting impression; also the day of the interview is so stressful that candidates may well not come across in their true light.

However, if only one day can be afforded for the final selection process then an informal reception and school tour should certainly be included both to allow the school to get to know the candidates and for them to get the feel of the school. In that sense it would be naïve for visitors not to realize that however informal the session it is none the less part of the assessment and selection process. It is often a good idea for this stage to be led by a senior member of staff who will not actually be on the interviewing panel, perhaps a deputy head who can then pass on any impressions gained.

The interview

Accepted practice is so strong in teaching that the selection process remains synonymous in most people's minds with a formal interview. So it is perhaps worthwhile reminding ourselves that this is not so in other walks of life. For a start it should be pointed out that the process is not necessarily any more protracted if candidates have a number of separate interviews with panel members. In the business world this is very much the rule and has the added flexibility of not requiring all the candidates at one time. For a profession which is all too often publicly judged by examinations, there is little attempt within it to examine professional skills via a prescribed task or in-basket exercise. Art teachers expect to bring their portfolios but should music teachers bring their instruments? Recently a drama post went to the candidate bringing a video of her current work to the interview!

At the formal interview the panel will be made up in accordance with school, governors and LEA guidelines but will vary enormously from place to place. Each teacher has a tale to tell on this score but personal experience has ranged from virtually the whole governing body for scale one to the head, chairman of governors and an inspector for senior teacher. However, what matters are the interviewing skills that are deployed by the panel members.

The initial questioning should be aimed at putting candidates at their ease and it may be some comfort to them to recall Cyril Poster's remark that 'The formal interview is without doubt the least important part of the proceedings when the candidates come to the school' (Cyril Poster 1976, p. 62). The physical arrangements of the room can easily, if unwittingly, add to the stress of the candidate, and a large panel membership is unlikely to help matters as well as limiting the time available to each member.

Having once settled the candidate in, the interview should aim to encourage a dialogue in which personal qualities and strength of character emerge, as much as an educational philosophy and an attitude to pupils. This will require skill and experience from the interviewers. Questions need to be succinctly worded – a long and involved question is very unlikely to succeed – and phrased so as to invite an open response capable of elaboration and development. Some actually amount to little more than a statement by the questioner while others pack two or three meaty separate issues in a grand composite question. Describing some hypothetical situation which the candidate is invited to deal with is extremely unlikely to prove helpful – teaching is about personalities and relationships. It is far better to build from common ground – thus 'A probationer is having difficulties; what advice would you give?' is not going to be as revealing as 'When observing a probationer what are you looking for?'

There will be areas of weakness that must be probed but a frontal assault will probably not achieve it. If a reference indicates a slackness with administrative matters then 'Do you keep to deadlines?' will not really help much. 'To what extent should teachers be judged by their administrative skills?' might be more use. Though that is not to deny a place for a straight question – 'Do you feel confident about teaching A level?'. But sometimes the straight question may be aimed at obtaining a commitment as a condition of appointment. In a strict legal sense this would be difficult to enforce, though clearly it would be unwise for a candidate to make a commitment lightly. There are also areas which should not be raised at interview; these include political and union affiliations and religion (except in the context of Church schools). Discriminatory questioning is also unacceptable with the criterion of would the same question be asked if the candidate were other than he/she is; for example, are all male candidates asked about their families' child-minding arrangements?

The composition of the panel may well predetermine the nature and quality of the interview. A candidate's professional qualities will be best examined by professionals – the headteacher, the adviser or the teacher governor. The lay panel members may well want to explore more general areas. A well chaired panel will have agreed in advance the way the questioning will be distributed. The time division for the simple arrangement of one question (plus supplementary) per member, especially common in the case of a large panel, is frequently counter-productive. One head was known to resort to issuing lists of suitable questions to lay panel members but surely the role of silent observer could allow them a detachment which could in fact be more valuable.

At the end of the round of questioning candidates should be given an opportunity to ask any remaining questions they might have. Given a reasonable initial introduction to the school there may well be none and certainly a question simply for the sake of it will do more harm than good. Also at the end of the interview – or sometimes at the beginning – candidates may well be asked whether, if offered the post, they are in a position to give a decision at once. This can sometimes be a surprise but reflects the fact that the school is anxious to get the post filled, while a candidate may have other interviews coming up and will wish to ask for time to consider. It is not uncommon for candidates still to be uncertain in their minds even after the interview. It is regrettable that LEAs will not pay expenses for candidates who honourably withdraw.

The appointment

Accepted practice in teaching is for all the candidates to wait around together during and after the interview. It is worth remembering that this is not so in many other walks of life and does, indeed, have certain disadvantages. If such waiting is to take place, a comfortable and reasonably secluded room needs to be provided and it is common for internal candidates to join the others at this point.

Meanwhile, the panel must move towards a decision. Some LEAs will expect their professional representative, the adviser or inspector, to sum up each candidate and present the confidential references obtained from other LEAs. Some panels try to find a consensus for eliminating the least favoured candidates at once and then concentrate on the remainder. Others will invite the opinions of staff who, though not present at the interview, conducted the earlier informal tour. It seems very unwise for a panel to push for a candidate who has not come across well to those who will be most directly concerned with that person's work, especially the head, and head of department, and for that reason such decisions are not properly the subject of a vote. If a consensus cannot be found it is almost certainly better not to appoint.

Once the panel are agreed on the successful candidate it is easy to have a sense of relief that all that is left is to offer congratulations. However, the recall of the chosen candidate is of crucial importance. The offer should be couched in the correct language as, in a legalistic sense, it forms a part of the contract. If in fact technically the panel's conclusion will form the basis of a recommendation to the LEA then 'I am pleased to offer you the post' is not right (though in a voluntary-aided school the governors may have this power). Equally it is necessary for the candidate to agree to accept the offer as made and, indeed, it is not unknown for the successful candidate to be overwhelmed at this point and decline the post or ask for time to consider. A further complication can be caused by the delay that will occur before the LEA confirms the offer as this may overrun the critical resignation date. Again, candidates who know that the offer will be subject to a satisfactory chest X ray within the last three years would be wise to have that done ahead so that they have a suitable certificate to hand.

In the excitement of concluding the appointment the unsuccessful candidates should not be forgotten. At the very least some general words of consolation should be offered and some heads feel it a professional duty to at least be ready to offer a word of individual solace and advice. There are, however, some occasions when this informality may have to give way to a formal record of why a candidate was rejected. This can arise during a reorganization when teachers may be allowed to challenge their rejection for certain posts. It can also be a wise safeguard if one of the candidates is already in dispute with the LEA over their terms of employment.

The contract

Throughout the process of seeking appointment and promotion it would be as well for the aspiring teacher to have in mind the nature of the various teacher contracts. Certainly when the offer made at the interview is confirmed by the LEA with a contract to be signed and returned, this should be studied fully. This is all the more important as LEAs increasingly offer temporary contracts and part-timers should investigate the employment protection available depending on the hours worked.

For the teacher the contract will reflect both national and local conditions of service. At present national conditions are set out in the 'Purple Book' though its exact status is still in doubt. There is strong pressure for a more precise definition of teachers' conditions of service as part of a general reappraisal of salary structures. Certainly the present situation does not match with the separate demands of the requirements of the Employment Protection (Consolidation) Act 1978. This requires an employee to receive in writing certain basic particulars about the terms of employment, for example, the title of the post and, interestingly, hours of work and holiday entitlement.

Details such as these given in writing in the contract constitute 'Express Terms'. It is not clear in law whether details given in advertisements or job descriptions are express terms. However, in so far as they clarify the general expectations placed on the post holder then they could well be seen as 'Implied Terms', and certainly such matters as satisfactory class control and lesson preparation in one's own time would seem to be implied terms even if not explicitly stated in such documentation.

Conclusion

A decision to apply for a post is a moment for taking stock. The teacher will feel that this is the right move at that time; the letter of application will force a self-appraisal of what has been achieved and what are the aims for the future. Equally the receipt of a request for a reference will mean the headteacher similarly appraising and predicting. It seems sad when these two tasks are not brought together and it also seems sad that the exercise will only be done for teachers on the move. For a school with a well established staff development programme as described in Chapters 6 and 8, it is extremely likely that the head and the teacher will have, perhaps annually, an opportunity to come together to evaluate performance and to set objectives for the future. In some cases this leads to the updating of an agreed open reference.

Such a programme should also allow the school a better insight into the way the variety of posts, each defined by its job description, actually come together as interrelating roles to create the organizational structure of the school. Thus the opportunities created by an impending appointment can be more exactly tailored to the needs of the school. It is certainly true that in the appointment of staff lies one of the most effective ways of raising the equality of the education of the pupils. A staff development programme is all the more necessary, in that it will build on the benefits of self-appraisal inherent in job application, at a time when falling rolls is severely limiting promotion.

Useful further references

ADAMS, N. (1983) *Law and Teachers Today*. Hutchinson.

BARRELL, G.R. (1978) *Teachers and the Law*. Methuen.

NATIONAL UNION OF TEACHERS (1981) 'Memorandum of appointment, promotion and career development'. NUT.

———— (1981) *A Fair Way Forward*. NUT.

POSTER, C. (1976) *School Decision-Making*. Heinemann Educational Books.

SECONDARY HEADS' ASSOCIATION Policy Statements Nos 23 and 27.

For an extended treatment of this aspect of school management tasks, see:

PAISEY, A. (1984) *Jobs in Schools*. Heinemann Educational Books.

4 Teacher Appraisal

Keith Blackburn

Perhaps the most difficult task for anyone in school management is to take responsibility for the work of another professional, and the most difficult part of that is to share perceptions of success and failure with that person. Our inclinations, training and experience as teachers do not help us with this managerial task: we are used to criticizing or blaming young people, but not assessing other professionals. The heart of the appraisal process is the special interview, and it needs careful consideration.

MM

The primary purpose of staff appraisal is to contribute to the professional development of teachers. Professional development has come more sharply into focus as the career opportunities for teachers have changed. Time was when their work was refreshed by movement to new posts and new schools. These changes were refreshing, both for the teachers who moved and for those who stayed and had to adjust to new working relationships. In new relationships lay the seeds of change which served to keep teachers' work alive and fresh: 'I've been in the school for ten years now, and I'm on my fourth head of department'. But the scene has changed. Increasingly teachers have to find their renewal within the existing roles. The use of various in-service training opportunities and the development of a working style which draws teachers into teams, rather than leaving them in isolation, each has an important part to play in this. So too does the *appraisal interview*.

This is an opportunity for teachers to have good work acknowledged and to gain the stimulation that comes from praise. Too often in schools the esteem in which teachers' work is held is left unspoken. To feel valued for the work that has been done motivates teachers to make future effort. More precisely there is the opportunity to recall the things teachers have specifically undertaken in the last year which, apart from having been beneficial to the pupils and the departmental team, have served to give the teachers areas of work through which they have found some sense of fulfilment.

51

For teachers busily engaged in the day-to-day work of the classroom there is the prospect of continuing to do the same things in the following year and in the years beyond that. The chance to pause and reflect through the appraisal process gives them the opportunity at least to question this ongoing cycle and to consider steps which would bring about change.

It is sometimes argued that in a team of teachers the working relationships that develop mean that appraisal is built into the ongoing work of the team, so a specific interview is an unnecessary extra in an already crowded programme. I would argue that there is value in having a point in the year both for the teachers and for the team when these three questions are posed and answered:

1 Where have we come from?
2 What is our present position?
3 Where are we going in the next year specifically and more generally in the years after?

Without the opportunity to pose these questions regularly, the tendency is for teachers to 'carry on' as before. Strengths are not acknowledged, weaknesses remain unremedied and new areas of work often remain unexplored. Regular review gives opportunity for teachers consciously to evaluate their work and plan for the future.

Who appraises whom?

The appraisal interview is a dialogue between two people in which the interviewer enables the teacher to become the active agent in his/her own appraisal. The process of the interview is crucially important. First, I want to consider the question of who should interview whom.

From the point of view of a school coming new to the appraisal process this raises two questions. In a developed system of staff appraisal, who will interview whom? In the meantime, what interim strategies will enable the school to arrive successfully at its long-term pattern?

In the long term it can be argued that the interviewer should be the person to whom the teacher is responsible within the structure of the school. This would give a pattern in many schools where:

> the headteacher interviews the deputy heads
> the deputy head (curriculum) interviews the heads of faculty or department
> the deputy head (pastoral) interviews the heads of year or house
> the heads of faculty or department interview the teachers who are members of their team
> the heads of year or house interview the tutors who are members of their team.

Under this arrangement, it is likely that most members of staff will be interviewed by at least two people, each focusing on different aspects of their work. Ideally, the heads of faculty or department will have had the opportunity to interview each of the members of their team before their own appraisal interview. For the head of faculty or department meeting the teacher, the agenda is the teacher's work as teacher. For his/her own interview, the agenda is extended to cover not only his/her own work as a teacher but also as a leader of a team of teachers. This will focus on what the team has achieved as well as his/her work in drawing out and extending the contribution made by each team member. It covers both the *task* aspects of the role as well as the *group maintenance* aspects (see Figure 4.1). So with the heads of year or house and with the deputy heads. They too need to meet for their appraisal interview when they have had an opportunity to see each of the members of the team for whom they are responsible so that they have the understandings and insights gained from these interviews to help them in looking at the various aspects of their own work.

It has been argued (Trethowan 1983) that confusion arises for the teacher in being responsible to more than one 'boss'. To resolve this, it is argued, each teacher should be seen as being responsible to *one* senior member of staff. The teacher's contribution to another area of the school – the pastoral team or the PE Department – should be negotiated through his/her head of department who would receive reports on the teacher's work and feed these into his/her own appraisal. Attractive as this suggestion might be in terms of resolving possible sources of conflict, it does not take account of the responsibility structures that actually exist in a good many schools. It

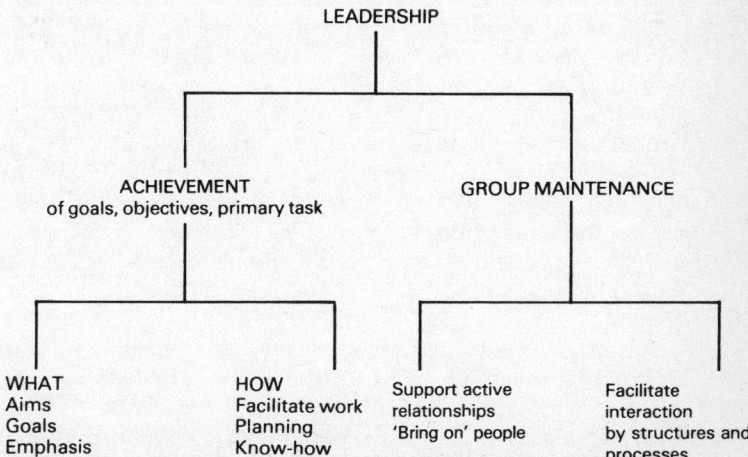

Figure 4.1   Aspects of leadership (reproduced from *Head of House, Head of Year*, Blackburn 1983, ch. 3)

would, for example, diminish the work of the heads of year or house in building up their teams if they did not have the chance to meet personally with each of the members.

Another possibility is for the headteacher to conduct all appraisal interviews. Whether this suggestion commends itself will depend on the underlying management philosophy being pursued. Where members of staff are being encouraged to take responsibility for their areas of work, the inclusion of staff appraisal interviews within their brief will enhance this. Where the headteacher is seeking to control the work of the school in greater detail, this aim would be served by his/her conducting the appraisal interviews.

Introducing an appraisal system

In the short term the introduction of an appraisal process has to be successfully negotiated. In particular, those who are going to conduct appraisal interviews need themselves to have been prepared for this. This will include discussion about the aims and objectives of the process. Most importantly, it needs to include experience of an appraisal interview. While in the long term it might be desirable to have seen all the teachers for whom the heads of faculty, department, year or house are responsible before they have their own appraisal interviews, in the short term there may be wisdom in arranging for these interviews to be held first so that senior staff have a working model of how to conduct such an interview.

There are two further ways in which a school might move towards a system of staff appraisal. The first is to use the device of an annual report. Heads of faculty or department and heads of year or house are asked to write a report on their work focusing on the three questions posed earlier: Where have we come from? What is our present position? Where are we going? This can be undertaken by the relevant heads themselves or be a collaborative exercise in which their team is involved. Discussion of the report then forms the basis of an interview which focuses on the team's work. Inevitably the discussion will range over the various contributions of team members and the contributions of the leader. The concrete focus of a report can help overcome some of the initial anxieties that can surround the introduction of an appraisal system (Blackburn 1983, Ch. 13).

A second strategy is to identify one or two faculties or tutorial teams and to start with them. The choice will be heavily influenced by those teams with whom it is expected it will be possible to work successfully. The headteacher or the deputy head will plan an initial programme of interviews, which may not reflect the intended final pattern, but which is designed to give a series of successful experiences to those who participate. Those who have participated will, no doubt, give their reactions to those who have not, and in this way the process is likely to become known to be a helpful experience. If the reverse happens, the development of an appraisal system will be severely hindered.

Such strategies will commend themselves differently in different schools. Out of this planning, the way forward in terms of introducing the system more widely among the staff is likely to suggest itself. Discussion of the process at a staff meeting, at team meetings, or through a circulated discussion paper, become a matter of timing within the overall strategy to bring about this particular development.

A good many teachers feel uncomfortable about the prospect of an appraisal interview. They may expect to be criticized, or assessed in a judgemental sense. Many teachers feel there are aspects of their work that could be better – but there is a limit to what the conscientious teacher can actually achieve. Such fears will only be dispelled through the *experience* of an appraisal interview.

The interview process exposes teachers to the possibility of being more open about themselves and their work than previously necessary in their working relationships. Whether teachers take that opportunity will depend in large measure on the skill of the interviewer, who needs to be ready to hear and to understand what is being said from the teachers' point of view, and to be able to empathize. The interviewer also needs to be able to see what might be realistically possible for particular teachers to achieve in the future. The interviewer may find the slowness of some irritating, the pushiness of others somewhat of a threat to his/her leadership. He/she has to be aware of his/her own reactions to individual teachers so as to convey an underlying acceptance of their worth to the work of the team. The process depends essentially on the building of a relationship of trust between the interviewer and the teacher through which the teacher actually experiences professional development. It is likely that in many instances a second appraisal interview will be more productive than the first, the third than the second.

It will also be true that the atmosphere of the appraisal interview will reflect the more general atmosphere in the school. Where teachers are working with pupils to help them appraise their own work and to set goals for themselves for their future work, they are already experiencing something of this same process. Where there are open discussions in teams of teachers about the content of the work and a realistic evaluation of what is being achieved which leads to modification of future work, then there is experience on which the appraisal process can build. It follows that in some schools the introduction of an appraisal process will be seen as a natural extension of other changes that have been taking place over a period of time. In other schools the possible introduction of an appraisal process is seen to be an agent of change which it is hoped will then feed into other aspects of the school's life. In some schools the introduction will be comparatively easy; in others much greater care will be needed to bring about its introduction successfully.

The appraisal interview

There are a number of basic conditions which need to be arranged for a successful interview. First, the teacher needs to be given due notice of the date and time of the interview so as to be able to prepare his/her thoughts beforehand. The place in which the interview is held needs to be conducive to giving attention to what each person is saying. The stock cupboard adjoining a noisy classroom will not be helpful. The arrangement of chairs will describe the relationship to be created – two equal easy chairs; seats either side of a desk. Sufficient time has to be allowed for the interview to be effective. For a good many interviews an hour will be needed; a half hour would seem to be a minimum. It also helps both participants if the time allocated is known before the interview starts. It is counter-productive if the teacher feels from the outset that at any point the interviewer might bring it to a close. It is possible, of course, that both will come to feel that the business has been concluded well within the allotted time span. It is also important that the interviewer arranges not to be interrupted during the course of the interview. The telephone can be a particular problem.

These conditions created, the interviewer and the teacher can attend to the process of the interview itself. This can be seen as falling into three phases.

1   Review

The teacher is asked to look back over a period of work and express his/her thoughts and feelings about what has been accomplished. Where have been the successes? Where have been the problems and difficulties? To what extent has the teacher been successful in achieving previously set goals? These questions have to do with *task*. He/she may also want to reflect on the working relationships that have been established within the team or teams of teachers to which he/she belongs. In talking he/she will be expressing, perhaps directly, perhaps indirectly, his/her feelings about the various roles that he/she undertakes. These issues have to do with the *group maintenance* aspects of the teacher's work.

The role of the interviewer in the first part of the review phase is to help the teacher articulate his/her thoughts and feelings. The interviewer will offer summaries of what the teacher is saying to check his/her understanding of what he/she hears. The teacher may confirm this or make another attempt to get across more precisely

what he/she means. The interviewer will reflect back to the teacher
the feelings that he/she discerns in what is said. He/she will draw
attention to areas of work in which the teacher feels successful and
thereby confirm the teacher's own perceptions of himself/herself.
The interviewer will also help the teacher express and clarify aspects
of the work in which the teacher feels that there are weaknesses. The
second part of the review brings in the interviewer's own perceptions
of the teacher's work. Apart from confirming successes and possibly
agreeing with identified weaknesses, there will be other matters that
he/she wants to include in the review. As the interview proceeds the
interviewer may well find that there are matters which concern the
teacher of which he/she was simply not aware. Equally, issues which
seem important to him/her may not figure in what the teacher says.
In these circumstances the interviewer has to decide whether there
will be profit in raising them or whether to wait. As he/she listens
and responds, the interviewer is giving weight to what the teacher
says by expressing agreement or by suggesting there is an over- or
under-emphasis.

The aim of the review phase is that the interviewer and the teacher
should come to some common understandings about the period
under review. Both have the opportunity to raise issues; both
contribute to the process.

2   The present position

From the review which has ranged over the year's work it is likely
that particular themes and emphases will emerge. The interviewer
shares in building the picture of the teacher's present position by
drawing together the threads that have run through the review
phase. In summary the interviewer confirms successes, agrees with
weaknesses and identifies where there are areas of disagreement
between himself/herself and the teacher. This provides the starting-
point for entering into the third phase of the interview.

3   Future aims and goals

In this phase the interviewer and teacher together establish an
agenda of issues and goals and come to a common understanding
about the order of priority. This phase needs to be specific, not
general, as in the following examples:

> The young teacher agreed that he/she needed to plan the process of each
> lesson with the fourth-year pupils in greater detail, writing blackboard
> summaries before the lesson began, preparing handouts for use during the
> lesson and being very clear about the homework tasks set.

> The recently appointed head of department, who felt there was much that
> needed changing, agreed that his/her first priority would be to review the
> work in the second year and that it would be important to draw other
> members of the team into this planning process, not only for this particular

piece of work but as a means of establishing a style of working which he/she would be able to use again.

The head of fourth year had recently become aware of an increase in absenteeism from classes during the day and planned a number of specific strategies to identify those who were absent.

The head of third year felt that the programme to help pupils with their choices of subjects had gone well this year and there was no particular need for changes. Next year, however, the majority of the tutors would be new to these procedures and careful planning would be required in order to repeat the previous success.

A deputy head of department, who had been applying unsuccessfully for promotion, was helped to plan a programme of reading and attendance at two in-service courses which it was hoped would compensate for areas of weakness that had been revealed in interview.

The planning of future aims and goals is specific. It will be possible in due course to make some estimate of success; indeed, the plans formulated at one appraisal interview form a basis from which the review phase of the next can begin.

The skill of the interviewer at this point lies in knowing which suggestions or possibilities are realistically within the scope of the teacher to achieve, when to encourage the teacher to be a little more adventurous and when to suggest some curbs on enthusiasm. It is important that the teacher is likely to be successful in the things that are planned. To place too little demand on the teacher is to leave him/her with a sense of being less than fulfilled in his/her work. To place too great a demand is to expose the teacher to unnecessary failure. The aim is to maximize the teacher's motivation and fulfilment through the work undertaken.

By the end of the interview both the interviewer and the teacher ought to have a clear understanding about the points that have been agreed between them. These can helpfully be written down so that both have a copy.

At the end of a successful interview teachers should feel that
1 There has been a basic acceptance both of them and their work
2 There has been a confirmation or a new understanding of areas of success
3 There has been a realistic understanding of areas of failure
4 A manageable plan for action has been formulated which will enable them to develop professionally
5 They have a renewed sense of their own value within the school and of commitment to its aims and goals, particularly those which affect their area of work.

The interviewer and the leadership role

For convenience so far I have used the word 'interviewer'. This may refer to the headteacher, a deputy head, a head of faculty or department, or to a head of year or house – to a number of people who exercise a leadership role within the school. The appraisal process gives any of these members of staff a specific opportunity to exercise their leadership of a team of professionals. In particular, it gives the leader the opportunity to contribute to the discussion about the shape that each team member's work will take. It is common when teachers are appointed for there to be a thorough exploration of the ways in which they would undertake the role for which they have applied. It may be that there will be some planned procedure to induct them into the school, during which the perceptions of both the leader and the teacher about the way the role will be carried out are further explored. At these points there is a high level of activity. From then on the interactions tend to be briefer, to be concerned with immediate issues or to be a response to a particular problem. Less often is there the opportunity afforded by the appraisal interview to look at the whole picture and to formulate plans for the future. The leader in this context has the opportunity to emphasize particular factors, to encourage particular developments in some directions and discourage them in others and to set the particular teacher's work in the context of other members of the team. In these ways the leader has the opportunity to help each member of the team see how his/her work and developing role dovetail into the contributions of others and how this will serve to forward the immediate and long-term plans for the team. In discussion questions will arise about the aims and goals of the school and the ways in which these are being implemented. Exploration of these issues will help the leader and the teacher to move closer towards a common understanding. It will also serve to bring out into the open issues where there is disagreement between them. Left unspoken, the opportunity may be missed to clarify misunderstandings and resolve felt differences. Where real differences exist, the work of the team is likely to be helped if these are acknowledged. More destructive is the undercurrent of opposition which the teacher feels is not heard because the leader has not provided the opportunity to listen.

Leadership involves mobilizing the members of the team in achieving the task. The appraisal interview gives the leader a unique opportunity to gain insights about team members – their ideas, their hopes, their fears and their limitations – and to plan work with them so as to maximize what each is able to offer to the achievement of the task. Held regularly they give him/her the chance to keep up to date with changes in the hopes and aspirations of those he/she leads. Alongside the daily work with members of the team and participation with them in meetings, the staff appraisal interview provides the leader with a key input to planning his/her own work, and to creating a sense of cohesion among team members.

References

BLACKBURN, K. (1983) *Head of House, Head of Year*. Heinemann
Educational Books.
TRETHOWAN, D. (1983) *Target Setting*. Education For Industrial
Society.

5 Working with Non-teaching Staff

Ian Leslie

Most teachers have very little support from other specialists in schools. The result is not only that many key aspects of a school other than teaching are less than well done, but also most teachers have had very little opportunity to consider the needs of other workers in schools or to practise working with them. Many large schools have undervalued and over-criticized office or caretaking staff at the same time as teachers have been dissatisfied with the support they are getting. Ian Leslie writes in the context of the Inner London Education Authority, who for long have been one of the few authorities endeavouring to provide appropriate levels and qualifications of non-teaching staff. How can the responsibility holder work best with them?

MM

In the popular image, a school consists of pupils and their teachers. In public discussion, education authorities are actually castigated for their wastefulness in employing other sorts of staff. The 'administrative and clerical' staff which an authority employs is commonly characterized as a bureaucratic burden on the system – with the plain implication that the education process would proceed more effectively, the more the ones who really mattered, teachers, were left alone to get on with it.

The facts are far otherwise. You, of course, realize perfectly well that you and your teaching colleagues could not even enter school on the first day of the year, much less continue, without the stage having been set by those working in many different sections of the council's service. Nevertheless, even for you it would be an instructive exercise to ask your school secretary for a full list of all the individuals, of all grades and types, who work daily just within your school. They may quite possibly exceed in number the teaching staff, and quite closely approach them even in the number of person-hours spent on the premises per year.

Because the formal interface between teaching and non-teaching staff rests in the person of the head and because decisions about the employment of non-teaching staff and the use the school makes of them will not often be made at any lower level than that of headteacher, it has seemed simpler to write this chapter as though addressed only to him/her. There is, however, an infinite number of informal points of contact at all levels of the hierarchy.

The very first point I should like to make is that every one of these people is able to affect the atmosphere and the efficiency of your school by the way they do their jobs and by the manner in which they relate to you, to other staff, to pupils and – since there will be many informal encounters – their parents. It would be inappropriately condescending to say that this is true 'even' of the most menial cleaner, working only before and after school is officially open. The pay and conditions of service of many of your workers define them as 'menial', and yet within the community of the school, many are capable of building personal and working relationships of great mutual value and of being helpful well over and above the level of their duties as defined on paper.

The *sine qua non* of this happening is that the individuals should know that their work – or even the very fact that they exist – is recognized and valued by those they serve. I ask you to consider spending the time it takes to meet all staff in turn, in *their* time at *their* place of work (not, of course, without first letting their immediate supervisor know what you are up to). Find out a little about their personal circumstances, where they live, whether they have other connections with the school (daughters or sons as pupils?) or other local schools, their prejudices and preferences, their own feelings about the school. Find out whether they know – by sight? by name? – the teachers who use the rooms they service, and arrange intro-ductions if they do not.

Non-teaching staff should also be invited to take part in the social life of the school. This may happen without any help from you, but it may not! Consider whether the process of integrating the non-teaching staff needs your active encouragement – or even waits to be initiated by you. If, sadly, you come to the conclusion that the latter is the case, you may well think it worthwhile to ask a colleague at deputy head or senior teacher level to take specific responsibility for a programme of teaching/non-teaching staff liaison.

Ancillary staff in schools fall into a number of distinct groups, each with different career structures, different terms and conditions, different contracts of employment. I shall give a brief conspectus of these groups before dealing in greater detail with the question of the administrative and clerical staff of the school office, the group who work most closely in tandem with you in the strategic management of the school. What I have to say in this section is true of schools run by the Inner London Education Authority. There will be differences elsewhere, but not so great as to invalidate my remarks as a general guide or to justify making detailed comparisons with examples from other education authorities. The main groups of ancillary staff are:

Schoolkeeping or caretaking staff

The schoolkeeper, the deputy and assistants, and their small army of cleaners 'go with the building', in respect of which, and so far as concerns *all* its users, the schoolkeeper is responsible for: cleanliness, maintenance, heating and ventilation, safety, security, liaison with other services, instruction, organization, and first-line supervision of his/her own staff. A schoolkeeper's path of promotion, having progressed from assistant to deputy to schoolkeeper, lies (not altogether unlike that of a teacher) in moving to larger and larger establishments and eventually possibly in becoming a supervisor of schoolkeepers, responsible for an area. Schoolkeepers are very conscious of their job as a career, constantly in touch with one another in the various schools, highly unionized, and, I think, very conscientious indeed. Second only to the head's *nominal* responsibility for everything, the responsibility schoolkeepers assume personally for the care and custody of the building and its major contents is real and wide-ranging. They have to know their building, its lighting and heating systems, its peculiarities, its weaknesses, its vagaries – but equally they have to deal competently with a substantial amount of record-keeping and form-filling, and, often the most demanding of skills, to be a master of alternate firmness and tact in managing their hard-worked and low-paid staff. The schoolkeeper is entitled to your consideration in such matters as giving enough notice of requirements outside routine. Give him/her more than just necessary consideration – *show* that you appreciate and value his/her work, and the schoolkeeper can give you help far beyond the call of duty.

Schoolkeepers are normally resident on the premises and responsible for them night and day; they must make explicit arrangements for their deputy to take over when they go on holiday. At the other end of the scale, the cleaners are paid for exact hours worked, hours which may be very inconvenient, perhaps starting at six in the morning. Their work is scrutinized in detail and other people's smallest acts of inconsiderateness (for example, a teacher's not making sure that chairs are placed on tables, where that is the agreed routine, or allowing things to be left lying on surfaces that have to be dusted) have the most direct and immediate effect on the difficulty of their task.

The school kitchen staff

An 'establishment within an establishment', the kitchen is staffed, funded and supervised quite independently of the school organization. The kitchen superintendent has a catering qualification, has supervisory support from an area office and expects to have with you the sort of relationship that other independent users of your premises have. Your responsibility to the kitchen superintendent rests entirely on 'your side of the serving hatch': you and your staff must see that the life and work of the kitchen staff are not adversely affected by the indiscipline of pupils. Beyond that, make friends with the kitchen staff and they are likely to give you lots of help and advice with catering for extra-curricular functions. Your perceived attitude to them can also make a very great difference to how they relate to the pupils. Ignore them, offend them, and at worst your school kitchen may restrict itself to its sole formal responsibility, the service of lunches. Take no one for granted. Obvious? Perhaps, yet worth repeating simply because the pressures of daily existence in a school make it very easy to ignore anything and anybody that is not positively demanding remedial attention!

Lunchtime supervisors

A group of staff engaged just for the midday period to help you supervise those pupils who stay in school to eat (on the assumption, the realism of which you will quickly assess, that the other pupils simply disappear from the site from the first to the last minute of the statutory lunch break). They need qualities of authority, charisma, understanding of children, coolness, tact and judgement such as possessed by few of the very best teachers, yet they receive one of the lowest rates of pay around. If you can recruit suitable, mature members of the local community who do not need the job(!) but have the time to spare, they can be pearls far beyond their price and will accept a responsibility towards your pupils that you would not require of a senior teacher! If you can recruit people whose ability is only commensurate with the pay and the overt status of the job as that of 'keeping an eye on the kids and stepping in to stop them doing anything too dreadful', but who at least are honest and reliable, then I suggest the best way to use them is as a team helping a designated senior member of the teaching staff. (This is provided you have such a colleague willing to undertake the task, which will be voluntary.) There should be extremely explicit instructions about the particular area they are required to supervise, what they should not permit, to whom to turn for help and where that person is to be found.

Technicians (science, art/pottery, design and technology)

This group of staff have pay and service conditions negotiated nationally and related to those of their counterparts in universities and other higher education and research establishments. They work to the specialities mentioned, under specialist heads of teaching departments who, with them, have the benefit of readily available advice from the education authority's specialist inspectors and advisory teachers. It is therefore in practice unnecessary, and could be seen as insulting and officious, for you to concern yourself directly with their work and its supervision. There is just one thing you should make perfectly clear: you are nominally responsible for reporting their absences, on leave or for other reasons, for purposes of adjusting pay, sickness benefits, etc. As it would be difficult or impossible for you or your school secretary to keep track of these matters directly, you should make it an explicit responsibility of each head of department to notify the school office promptly of the absence or return of any of their technicians. (The same is true of a unique person, the home economics ancillary. HE ancillaries do for the HE department very much what laboratory technicians do for science, but they are not formally qualified, are not clearly part of any group to look after their interests, and are low paid.)

General assistants

An odd category of staff employed on an hourly rate of pay in term-time only whom you might well employ to assist supervision at other times than the lunch hour – to take charge of the medical room and assist the visiting doctor and nurse at medical examinations; to assist with office processes not requiring clerical skills, like working the duplicator, etc.

Librarian; media resources officer (MRO)

To include these two as 'non-teaching' staff at all is hardly more than a technicality. Both professionally trained and highly selected, they will not fail to involve themselves directly with teacher colleagues in matters of curriculum and syllabus, and from your side you would do well to involve them in curricular consultations at head of department level. It would be appropriate, for instance, to invite them to heads of department meetings. As teachers will by now be using the various media inextricably and almost interchangeably, encourage to the fullest extent cooperation between your librarian

and your MRO and do your best to provide the physical conditions
for their two departments to work together. When a teacher requires
a videotape, some books and a photographic collection to illustrate a
section of a course it would be unfortunate if they had to be ordered
separately and fetched from different parts of the building.

Administrative/executive and clerical staff; the school office

You *could* run the school organization without the school office and
other clerical help. About the only things that you virtually must
have administrative/clerical staff to do are pieces of administration
laid down in a hard-and-fast way by your authority's central
administration, such as the notification in specific ways of details of
pupil roll, staff records and payments, 'casualty returns' of staff
absences, and the handling and recording of cash income and
expenditure. The idea of the teacher, uniquely among all the staff of
a school, being a Jack-and-Jill-of-all-trades dies hard. I have just
seen a circular which, in the course of worrying about the poor
maintenance of school minibuses, tells heads to see that 'a single
named *teacher* [sic – my italics] is given responsibility for checking
that the vehicle is regularly serviced and the records are kept up to
date'. Now to assume that the most suitable person in a school to
take on the task of vehicle maintenance management is a teacher is
surely to stretch beyond reason the concept of teachers' universal
proficiency. Moreover, although in practice you might perfectly well
find that one of your staff has the necessary abilities for the task,
there are other aspects of running a minibus for the school that make
a teacher, tied to a timetable, the least suitable person. There has to
be a booking system, an adjudication of priorities where booking
requests clash, an agreed place to pick up and return the keys; the
'transport manager' needs to be free during the normal working day
to take the vehicle for servicing. Moreover, it is undesirable that the
provider of such a coveted service as the loan of the minibus should
be associated with any particular section of the academic body. Such
considerations, I suggest, mean that the job does not require a
teacher's particular skills but does require a person free of the timetable's demands and working generally in a fixed base.

   That is only an extreme example of the many non-teaching tasks
that may, if that is how you choose (or if it is how you have to work
because your education authority offers you no choice), be done by
teachers but could alternatively be taken off their hands by ancillary
staff. Carried out by teachers they will be done with varying degrees
of effectiveness because they need skills other than those for which
teachers are selected and in which they have been trained. Getting
them done at all will rely heavily on gratuitous goodwill, with the

corollary that it will be difficult to apply pressure, let alone sanctions, when they are not done well. Continuity of style, or even of the voluntary undertaking itself, will be a matter of sheer accident when staff changes take place. As regards tasks that have to be undertaken in a number of places in the school (correspondence with parents, to take just the most obvious example), it will be impossible to secure consistency in the most elementary aspects of 'house style'.

May I move from the one extreme, where even a demonstrably unsuitable task is expected to be carried out by a member of the teaching staff, to an imaginary opposite position – which we are unfortunately most unlikely to see in this country's schools – before moving on to consider to what extent you might not unreasonably approach it in practice? (I would add that it is not unrepresentative of what you would find in a business establishment disbursing comparable total costs and with a staff population of similar size!)

A comprehensive school so staffed as to give a ready and effective service to parents and to leave the head and other teachers free to devote their time to the use of their professional skills would, I suggest, have a central office sufficiently staffed to provide, in conjunction with staff working under the MRO on specialist reprographics, a full service for the typing and duplicating of all but the most trivial items of correspondence, internal agendas, minutes and discussion documents, and classroom materials, and to give full clerical support to the routine parts of school practices and procedures such as the collation and despatch of pupil reports, the arranging of career interviews, medical examinations, pupil admission procedures, and so on.

A member of the office staff (or rather a rota of them covering times well straddling the school's official opening hours) would at all times be acting primarily as receptionist, able, with the support of internal training and the ready availability of timetables, etc., to respond readily and appropriately to the many and varied requests for information and assistance received every day at a school from parents of present, past and prospective pupils, from neighbours, from other professionals, or from any member of the public.

It goes without saying – no, I admit it does not, but it should – that the head responsible for a staff numbered in three figures and pupils numbered in four ought to have a personal assistant able to: deal with all callers and telephone calls directly concerning the head when they arrive during that greater part of the day which he/she certainly should be spending elsewhere than in his/her office; organize the head's appointments, travel arrangements, and so on; advise and generally smoothe the way in all matters of the head's contacts with all sections of the local authority and other services; type, or supervise the typing of, all the head's correspondence and deal with its filing, the sending of appropriate information copies, 'chasing', and so on.

The head's deputies might well share the services of another such person, and although the section staff (heads and deputy heads of houses or years, mini-school coordinators or whatever the particular school has) may not need such personal support, still each section base or headquarters surely should have its own clerical assistant to take messages and arrange appointments as well as to type and organize correspondence and other documentation and take full responsibility for record-keeping.

It follows from the very nature of the teacher's timetable dominated day that some at least of the staff working in each of these ancillary capacities need to be present from well before until well after classrooom hours, so that ideally some of the individuals specified above would need to be pairs working early and late with an overlap.

In considering the use of office staff to free teachers, I would ask you first to notice what a large proportional increase in office staffing is possible in exchange for a small proportional reduction in other resources – where the matter is open to choice.*

For example (London 1983–84 figures, slightly rounded): A school of 1600 pupils is allocated a teaching staff basic establishment of 120. The cost of employing these teachers (averaged across scales and including N.I. and administrative costs) is a fraction under £1.14 million. The basic establishment of office staff for this school costs, in the same terms, £55 000 (an Admin B, an Exec 1, two Clerical 1, 26 hours clerical term-time only, 90 hours general assistants term-time only). The cost ratio is just about 21 to 1: ancillary help spread very thin!

The head of this school now has to decide how to allocate his/her cash resources (around £175 000, in the same example) among the alternative spending heads. Smaller teaching class sizes? A reduction of average class size from 25 to 22.5 in the first three years of 300 pupils each, assuming average teaching load of 20 periods in a 25-period week, would require 5 extra teachers at a cost of nearly £50 000. The same cash amount would permit just about a doubling of the office staff establishment (more than doubling the hours of

---

*In ILEA schools, a virement scheme known as AUR (Alternative Use of Resources) allows heads, subject to certain limitations and after consulting their staffs, to choose how to allocate resources (made up of a per capita school allowance and a roughly equal further amount, expressed as a cash total) among the following broad heads of expenditure: (a) teaching staff additional to the establishment allocated by the authority; (b) non-teaching staff, again additional to a basic establishment; (c) school allowance to be spent on books, materials and pupils' amenities; and (d) minor building works. Heads in authorities without an institutionalized virement scheme would no doubt have to persuade their chief education officer's staff to put any proposed virements into effect, but it should be possible in the end.

identifiable help to particular parts of the teaching organization, if you extract as a constant the school secretary and deputy, much of whose time is pre-empted by unavoidable administrative and supervisory tasks).

Of course I do not for one moment suggest that the planning of teacher disposition is ever based on such crude equations, or that gross alternatives of this sort are ever, in the real world, open to a head at one point in time. I do hold, however, that even so crude a comparison as I have made is valid as a factor to be taken into account in deciding the general direction of policy. Clerical help *for clearly-defined uses* is a very good bargain.

Another example from real life, the exact details softly blurred: consideration is being given to timetabling one full-length period per week for each tutor group in which to treat, more fully than registration time ever allows, those matters that tutoring is all about, and for these periods to support each tutor by an additional teacher, both to work together to a personal development syllabus that will bring in the specialisms offered by the additional teacher in each case.

At the same time, heads of houses are bemoaning the fact that, because of cuts caused by reduction of resources at a time of falling rolls, they have lost something they used to have: a few specified hours each of the services of a clerical assistant. This assistant used to report to each house room in turn to do their filing, typing for the house heads who did not prefer to do their own, and general tidying up of records.

The total extra teacher-time required for the modest curricular proposal, for only the lower three years, of 300 pupils each in tutor groups of 25, is 36 periods or, in a 25-period week, 1.8 teachers, at a cost of £17 000. If this sum is spent instead on term-time only clerical help, it will buy almost exactly a hundred hours per week, which would give every one of ten houses/years two hours each day of their very own dedicated clerical assistance.

At a more uncomplicated level, you might be comparing the benefits of £350 in your budget for books against the possibility of employing one of your part-time clerical assistants for an extra two hours a week for a year and setting that time aside specifically for the duplication of classroom worksheets.

If, as plainly I am advocating, one of the things you expect of your school office and MRO's organization is a reprographic service open to the whole school, you need to insist that they have a clear-cut system for accepting and fulfilling orders – and also for raising charges against the school allowance allocations of the respective departments. Standard forms are an almost indispensable adjunct to efficiency here. You may have to sell this idea to a great many teachers, who in good faith think of filling in forms as something demanded by bureaucracies in the outside world but which ought to have no part in exchanges between colleagues in the friendly school community. In practice, without an explicit ordering system you will find a gross imbalance in the use of office facilities and the satisfaction they give, according to which teachers have the gift of 'charming' the workers in the office. Nothing very complicated is needed, and a more generally happy atmosphere results from a system that is seen to be fair and reliable, than from any amount of inappropriate informality. As regards charges, I strongly recommend that these be made, and debited to departmental shares of the teaching materials allowance. If this is not done it is certain that disproportionate use will be made of the facility by a minority of departments as a gratuitous boost to their allowances, at the expense of those least skilled at using the service or for whom home-made materials are least appropriate. The cost of the office staff and stationery is, after all, borne by the school budget as a whole.

It is quite easy for the school secretary to draw up a list of charges based on the cost of materials plus, say, 5 per cent for wastage, and a notional charge for labour. Each teacher ordering work fills in a simple form, which should state:

> Number of copies
> Special instructions (for example, print on card; single/double sided; coloured paper)
> Department to which cost is to be charged
> Date of handing in work
> Date work must be ready

The form should be duplicated on a distinctive coloured paper (so as not to get misplaced among other pieces of paper) and made readily available in the staffroom as well as the school office.

I cannot stress too srongly the importance of recording the two dates mentioned above. The flow of work into the office from a multitude of teachers in many departments is highly uneven. In general, the more notice given, the more even the flow of work can be through the office. You and the school secretary should therefore do everything possible to encourage teachers to think ahead. However, whatever you do they will often leave things late. To ask for work to be done 'immediately' is unrealistic – it will be an unusual day on which anyone has not got some piece of work already in hand. To ask for it 'as soon as possible' – although this is in fact one of the commonest forms of request! – is virtually meaningless. Everyone else may be asking the same thing and your item required 'as soon as possible' ends up somewhere in a queue *after* the only piece of work given an explicit deadline, even though that piece may not really have been so urgent. If each piece of work has a deadline, it is easy for the office manager to assess a couple of days ahead of time whether there is going to be any difficulty and to let the 'customers' know the situation. Stating the date of ordering gives a simple basis for deciding on priorities should there be too much work to get through at a particular time.

You can use your clerical staff to facilitate the tactical details of processes whose meaningful content is wholly a teacher's professional affair. I give just one example: reports. In my own schooldays the report was a single sheet with one line per subject on which the subject teachers each entered as much as six words . . . for an interesting pupil. More and more schools now use separate subject sheets, with copies for house/year and subject department records, and an overall remarks sheet for the tutor and perhaps the house/year head. It was quite satisfactory to have each subject teacher pass on their batch of those single sheets to the next, when they met as they regularly did in the smaller staffrooms of a generation ago. Nowadays, you can set a final deadline for the despatch of a year's reports and leave it to the teachers, and I wish you luck. Or you can set and publish a systematic schedule, using the clerical staff to do the boring bits systematically, like this:

From 14 Dec: subject report forms ready for collection from school office.
By 9 Jan: subject teachers return reports to school office. Office staff:
  Gather the reports into sets by tutor group
  Sort into alphabetical order within tutor groups
  Separate alphabetical sets into three copies
  Send house/year copies and subject department copies, in sets, to appropriate section heads
  Provide correct number of 'tutor's overall remarks' report form, and same number of correct size envelopes.
11 Jan: Tutors collect ordered report sets from school office.
18 Jan (i.e. after a weekend): Tutors hand completed reports to pupils and return those for absentees to school office whose staff (forewarned by schedule to set aside staff time) address and post them on same day.

I should like to elaborate a little on the important role of the receptionist. In the business world, an establishment anything like as big and complex as a secondary school has a trained tele-phonist/receptionist always on duty. Your budget is unlikely to allow you to treat this as a separate post; the job will have to be fitted in with the other work of your office staff and, as I have suggested, it is probably best done on a rota. If you can persuade staff to stagger their hours of attendance, it should be possible for the switchboard and reception window to be staffed continuously for a substantially longer stretch than the school day. This is very necessary because probably the majority of staff contacts with visitors, especially with parents, have to be made before and after teaching time. It is most undesirable that parents and other visitors should have to find their way in to the school, or that telephone callers should have to take their chance with a night extension system.

The vital thing about reception is that each member of staff during their turn at this duty should clearly understand that it takes full priority over other tasks. They must feel supported in this position if other work which it was hoped they could do at the same time falls behind. Nothing could be a surer recipe for dissatisfaction and inefficiency than uncertainty over who is to leap up to answer the telephone or go to the reception window. Either everyone leaps up at once or no one moves for what seems ages, and all day no one is quite able to concentrate on what they are doing at their own desks.

It is impossible to over-stress the symbolic importance of the way visitors are received – its friendliness, its appropriateness of style, and its effectiveness – in giving them their first impression of the school. You must see that your teaching colleagues understand this and use the office reception function fully. The most alert, welcoming, trying-to-be-helpful receptionist cannot undo the impression of uncaring created when a visitor arrives to keep an appointment made with a teacher, only to find they are apparently unexpected because the person who made the appointment has not told the school office.

This is another instance – and many more will occur to you for your particular school – where the use of a simple standard form in another distinctive colour is the most helpful and effective way of doing things. The 'Reception of Visitor' form should state: name and status of expected caller; date and time expected; where host staff member will be waiting (plus phone extension). To be greeted by a friendly 'Can I help you?' is a big improvement on having to knock and wait for attention, or stand wondering whose attention to gain, but 'Hello, I expect you are Mr Smith. Ms Brown is expecting you, I'll phone and let her know you are here', is the sort of reception we should really aim to offer.

Again, you will probably not be able to afford a full-time personal assistant to anybody; but I suggest that a certain amount of specific allocation of assistance is a great aid not only to efficiency but to job satisfaction for the office staff. You and the school secretary may agree, and make it clear to all, that the prior duty of all the office staff is to the general administration of the school. Certainly it is as true that every member of an office staff in school at one time or another has a go at every sort of job there is to do, as it is that there are times when all of them will be mucking-in together at some single big job with a deadline to meet. But at least it is possible to specify that, in the absence of particular reasons to the contrary, A does the mathematics work, B types and files the head's correspondence and keeps his/her appointments, and so on. (At the simplest level, this ensures that someone gets to know the vagaries of different staff members' handwriting, spelling weaknesses, and so on, and improve accuracy of output!) Often, individual preferences can be respected while carrying out this process of allocation.

Do not think this a hopeless counsel of perfection just because you see no chance of employing as much ancillary staff as you would like.

I have seen a deputy head with responsibility for coordination of a house system, and four house rooms each with a head and a deputy head of house, all rendered a service they considered invaluable (and confirmed they had found it so when they lost it) by one basic-grade clerical assistant employed for 20 hours a week in term-time only. She was able to take more off the hands of the teaching staff than the count of hours suggests, because she could concentrate uninterrupted on the filing, typing and updating of records. Teachers can rarely do this in peace unless they stay well after hours, by when their enthusiasm for such tasks tends to have flagged.

In dealing with your office staff, and in deciding how much you expect of them, you should bear in mind that they are employed on a very different basis from teachers. While the main teachers' organizations are still resisting the introduction of detailed contracts of service and the teacher's only specific attendance requirement is to be present during the $27\frac{1}{2}$ hours of timetabled time for 39 weeks a year, their *un*specified commitment is open-ended. During term-time many of them will be in school working in a number of ways that are fully a teacher's work although not in front of a class, well before opening time and on into the evening. Administrative, executive and clerical staff on the other hand work to a career structure and conditions that are, on paper, the same as those of thousands who work in other establishments of the local authority. There the work is normally organized in much larger staffing units divided into specialized sections, in which the clerical staff work at an ordered pace with few interruptions and almost no contact with the public. Among other relevant matters, their contractual hours of work are very exactly specified, for example:

> the standard working week is 35 hours per week. The normal hours of attendance are Monday to Friday, 8.45 a.m. to 4.30 p.m., with a lunch break of 45 min. They have the choice, however, of working the above standard week or working a $36\frac{3}{4}$ hour week making a standard day of 8.45 a.m. to 4.51 [sic!] p.m. with the extra time accrued to earn one of the following options:
> a reduction of $3\frac{1}{2}$ hours in the length of each of two working days per calendar month; or one day off each calendar month.

They also have carefully specified entitlements of annual leave, according to length of service.

You will find school office staff get very personally involved in the work and ethos of a school and you will rarely find them insisting on working exact hours, but when you do sometimes expect a little more of them it is well to bear in mind what the basic requirement is. If you encounter a high degree of commitment resulting in, for example, a willingness to stay for after-school activities in term-time, do not take it for granted. Do not make the mistake, either, of acting as though you assume that staff described as 'all-year-round' (in contradistinction to term-time only staff) are literally there throughout the year taking no holidays. If you are tempted to leave large chunks of drafting and other work until the holidays because that is when you will be free of minute-by-minute term-time pressures, remember that each all-year-round person is entitled to, as well as all the statutory bank holidays, perhaps five or six weeks leave, nearly all of which they will be taking during the school's total of thirteen weeks closures. Thus there is a low limit to how much they can undertake in the school holidays, even if they did not have to spend some of their time doing the daily routine things that in term-time are done by the more junior term-time staff. Remember also that they too work under considerable pressure in term-time and will appreciate a more relaxed work experience in the school holidays.

6　Staff Development

Colin Bayne-Jardine

Overall the education manager's main task for which skill is needed is to help his/her staff develop their skills. Helping staff development is, of course, not a single discrete skill. Rather it is the bringing together of a whole range of skills. To the teacher used to working with young people this may appear daunting, or, as Colin Bayne-Jardine argues, it could be regarded as part of the educational ambition.

MM

It is fundamental that no system can develop people nor can one person develop another. All personal development is self-development and this takes place when people use the opportunities available to increase their skills, knowledge, competence and confidence. It is the task of heads and senior staff in schools to create a climate in which people can grow. A supportive yet challenging working atmosphere is one of those things that is easy to say but difficult to provide. 'It is easier and less contentious to talk about professional development in terms of structures, frameworks, resources and methods, rather than in relation to desirable forms of personal knowledge and understanding.' (Taylor 1980, p. 338.) In this chapter I shall try to get at the substance of school-based staff development rather than suggest a formula or system, and begin by attempting to clear the ground. All too often this subject is covered in a tangled growth of misunderstanding and false expectations.

'There was only one catch and that was Catch-22 which specified that a concern for one's own safety in the face of dangers that were real and immediate was the process of a rational mind.' (Heller 1962, p. 46.) In Joseph Heller's novel there is a 'spinning reasonableness' in Catch-22. Orr, a member of a bomber crew, was clearly crazy and could be grounded. He simply had to ask but as soon as he did so he was acting rationally and would have to fly more missions.

All too often when discussing staff development people avoid the implications of a school policy by pointing out the 'Catch-22' that apparently emerges between the objectives of a staff development policy in individual terms and those in organizational terms. A member of a school staff might wish to go on a course to develop skills, build on personal interests and prepare for promotion. The head of the school decides that the proposed course is not in the interests of the school. The member of staff either accepts the demands of the school and begins to feel frustrated and gradually begins to stop growing in the job, or goes on the course risking the hostility of the head which, in turn, could reduce his/her chances of further development.

Staff development is very often seen in such terms – individual teachers constructing their own programme in a competitive manner often in conflict with ill-defined school needs. This is a caricature of staff development, but it highlights the need for an approach which recognizes and relates the objectives of a staff development policy in individual terms with the objectives of such a policy in school terms. If staff development is seen in individual competitive terms there will be little of it because few teachers will ruthlessly exploit the process in their own interests. They may well feel frustrated but they will accept the stated demands of the school. Teachers gain a loyalty to their colleagues and their school, and the pull of the organization is strong. In such a context it is vital for a school to encourage personal growth and the development of professional skills. The reconciliation of the objective of helping teachers do their jobs more effectively with the objective of increasing the capacity of their school to cope with change is vital. It can be achieved by adopting a staff development approach or 'learning process' (Light 1973, p. 9).

There is also considerable confusion over the meaning of staff development. It is sometimes seen solely in terms of the provision of in-service education and training. INSET is not a synonym for staff development policies. Although it reduces complex issues too much, it is helpful to regard staff development as the over-arching concept and INSET as the main way in which development can be encouraged. It will be an empty exercise if schools simply publish an outline of their in-service activities without engaging teachers in the planning of the programme. Staff development along with much school-focused INSET (Bolam 1982) must be rooted in schools. It will become an essential part of a school's approach as 'an activity which is natural and occurs automatically as part of the management process'. (Hoyle 1973, p. 9.) It is important and worthwhile. As Denys John pointed out: 'A head who regards the growth and learning of all members of the teaching staff together as his most important objective is perhaps achieving the fulfilment of those aspirations which first made him choose education as a career and which became a habit of mind during his years as an assistant teacher.' (John 1971.)

Schools are people places. The process of teaching is carried out between people and any school organization depends on networks of human relations. Such an organization is best comprehended using the framework of open-system theory (Katz and Kahn 1978). This means that any policy will be changing as it interacts with the system. No school can remain static. There is an increasing pressure from the government and from the public for quality within the education system. Falling rolls and new curriculum expectations in a changing society make demands. A head cannot hope to cope without the active support of a team of professionals. The 'Catch-22' argument, and lack of clarity about the process, must not be permitted to squelch efforts to provide a school approach to staff development.

Traditional strategies are inadequate. These strategies could be outlined under three headings: *drift, direction*, and *demand*. *Drift* is a policy of 'laissez-faire', rooted in a belief in professional autonomy and the honing of skills on the stone of experience. Mr Chips would be an example of the product of such a policy. *Direction* is the policy rooted in the belief that it is really somebody's responsibility to organize a teacher's career. The development of the role of professional tutor sometimes carried the impression that staff development demanded control. Some of the staff appraisal programmes being produced sound directive and it is interesting that the Open University third-level course on management and the school has a course guide: *The Management of Staff* (1981). Finally, there is a policy of response to *demand* – the policy that emerges from the belief that every teacher has a professional right to further qualifications and these are seen as the main measured method of staff development. This approach can be found in the James Report third cycle (1972).

Many schools have evolved a response to demands for a stated staff development policy by mixing these three strategies, and such a mix cannot be effective because it will lack coherence and can be exploited by ruthless individuals. The James Report stressed the key part played by schools in the 'third cycle'. The place for staff development must be in the schools themselves. The whole approach of school-focused INSET (Bolam 1980) is in harmony with the strategy of the fourth 'D'-development.

This development strategy must be seen as an integral part of the school management structure. It must be built-in and not added on. The climate of the school (Miles 1965) must be right if the organization is to be healthy and flourish. The areas for review in any school are thus: communication flow, effectiveness of meetings, clarity of goals, avoidance of role conflict and opportunities for group problem-solving. In terms of a school organization all teachers must know their place in the team from the outline of the organization structure. They must know the main expectations of

Approaches to staff development

Rate the *extent to which you adopt* each of these approaches as follows:
5 = Very Extensively; 4 = Extensively; 3 = To a small extent; 2 = Very rarely;
1 = Never

1 Staff have opportunities for the development of leadership through the exercise of responsibility	
2 Staff are helped to develop problem-solving and decision-making skills	
3 Staff participate in decision-making on significant issues which affect them	
4 Staff interaction and communication are facilitated by organizational structures and processes	
5 Staff are encouraged to experiment and initiate change	
6 Counselling is provided to allay staff feelings of anxiety and to improve self-confidence	
7 Staff are encouraged to exchange ideas and information	
8 Staff are given clear understanding of roles and responsibilities	
9 Staff are given a clear understanding of school objectives and policies	
10 Staff ability to accept new challenges and experiences is developed	
11 Staff have opportunities to communicate their problems	
12 Staff engage in self-evaluation of school effectiveness	
13 Staff contributions and opinions are fully recognized and respected	
14 Staff are encouraged to participate in in-service education	
15 Staff evaluation is used primarily as a means towards self-evaluation and self-direction	
16 Staff meetings are used as a means of cooperative problem-solving and shared decision-making	
17 Staff working parties plan and experiment with new projects	
18 The school acts as an agent of in-service education for the staff	
19 Staff are provided with a professional library	
20 Staff are given a sense of purpose and commitment to common goals	
21 There is a carefully planned programme of induction and guidance for new teachers	
22 Staff talents are discovered and fully utilized	
23 Important decisions and responsibilities are delegated to staff	
24 Staff are given a sense of professional worth and self-respect and achievement	
25 Staff are given opportunities to develop their special interests	
26 Staff values, opinions, feelings and needs are respected	
27 The general climate of the school encourages openness, security and trust	
28 Staff are fully consulted before the introduction of changes	
29 Staff attend refresher courses during school time	
30 Staff are helped to realize their professional career aspirations	

Figure 6.1

them from a job description and must feel that they receive explicit positive feedback on their performance. They should also feel that there are opportunities for development and that planning within the school is a cooperative venture. It is sometimes helpful to check the existing climate of a school by using a questionnaire, an example of which is given in Figure 6.1.

One school set about opening up the whole area of staff development by using a questionnaire with an arresting cover, and a light humorous touch. If the approach is too formal many staff may be very wary of becoming involved in the exercise and retreat behind a barricade of entrenched prejudices.

It is important that such questionnaires are completed by several members of staff so that the perceptions of senior staff can be seen in context. If a school is to adopt a school staff development strategy, it must provide a productive atmosphere which involves nearly everyone in developmental activities (Joyce 1980). It may be that a school decides that a mix of direction and response to demand will answer their situation, but to make full use of the resource of the staff a developmental approach will be more productive. Such an approach will only work in the appropriate open climate within the school.

Once the school has moved towards the use of the developmental strategy then there is the problem of how such a strategy can be implemented. A variety of approaches can be used and schools can adapt the approach chosen to their own situation. The start must be to focus on need and a useful model is one produced by M. Beeby and M. Broussine at Bristol Polytechnic. This gives the stages of problem-solving as follows:

1 Problem formulation
2 Producing proposals for solution
3 Forecasting consequences, testing proposals
4 Action planning
5 Taking action steps
6 Evaluating outcomes.

It is necessary to take time over the stage of problem formulation and of producing proposals for solution. Time will be needed for a group to settle down to work together and to trust each other. The stages are, of course, interlinked and the process is continuous and dynamic.

A school can bring awareness of staff development as an integral part of the work of the school by using well-respected, positive and adaptable leaders to set in motion a discussion on the needs of the school (Oldroyd, Smith and Lee 1984). The discussion of needs may take time and it is vital that it is a genuine discussion and not simply a method of direction. One school has attempted to define this sort of approach in the staff handbook as follows:

Management and delegation

Management should relate to harnessing enthusiasm, to an enabling process rather than formally defining a hierarchical framework. Delegation is essential not only in practical terms but as an expression of teamwork and partnership and as a process of staff development and training. Each staff member needs to feel part of a school beyond the classroom role. Delegation makes the management process more human and in order for it to work in a convincing fashion very clear communication is required. Senior staff and middle management have a vital role in developing views, ideas and initiatives. They need to stimulate and enhance real participation.

Once the needs emerge then the school can consider the repertoire of methods for helping staff development. There are a number of facilities and procedures which are related mainly to information. An INSET notice-board, a staff library, and sharing of information from courses attended are the sort of things that relate to this area. There is a further set of activities which involves groups of staff by virtue of their shared interests. A school induction course for probationers, a departmental handbook, departmental meetings to consider curriculum development and pastoral team meetings to consider specific problems, are all examples of such group shared interests. Clearly individuals can be encouraged and helped to work effectively together in groups and to draw on the skills of the group by making everybody aware of the developmental nature of the job in schools by good information and open communication.

Most people have fairly fixed patterns of management that match their personalities. The best way in which staff can learn to work more effectively and develop management skills is to bring the process of running a school into the open. Teachers are highly skilled and often underestimate themselves and avoid tackling new tasks by claiming that the organization around them works in a mysterious way. One important way to bring about a positive school climate is by opening up the management process. For example, many schools will give the task of staff welfare and development to a head of department or head of year. He/she is expected to take on this task for his/her team of teachers with little discussion as to the nature of the process. Too often the exercise becomes a sterile appraisal of weaknesses rather than a search for strengths. No mechanistic ritual of going through check-lists will help people develop. Time is needed to discuss, reflect and develop more successful patterns. Heads of department and others responsible for groups of colleagues must be encouraged to transform meetings from routine administration meetings to training and development sessions. This requires help and support from senior colleagues and an open discussion of the purpose of meetings. School committees can also be used for training and development. Papers on topics of interest to the school staff as a whole can be presented and discussed at such meetings which must be clearly separated from routine administration meetings. Senior colleagues can be given opportunities to chair discussion meetings, and nothing brings people together more than working together on a problem. After all people gain a vested interest in the solution if they are involved in this way. Participation in decision-making is one of the vital components of a school climate in which staff will learn to develop their skills. Not all matters are dealt with appropriately in such a way, hence the need to clarify which meetings are for discussion and which for administration.

Increasingly there is a feeling in the teaching profession that staff development is pointless because there are fewer promotion opportunities. This frustration arises from an acceptance of the demand strategy approach to staff development and there are ways in which opportunities for individual development can be created provided that the school climate is open enough and that people trust each other. It is possible to renegotiate a job description so that an individual is given a new area in which to work. A head of year could be given a curriculum responsibility to oversee fourth-year choice, for example. Furthermore, there could be an exchange of roles between, say, a head of department and a head of house. Such changes will require careful and sensitive handling but they can be valuable ways of encouraging individuals to develop new skills and must be linked to in-service support from outside the school.

One of the most exciting results of a developmental approach is when the whole staff works on an agreed task. This will not happen all the time, as the curriculum roundabout must turn and cannot be stopped for servicing. However, it can only happen in a school which is pursuing a policy using the developmental strategy. An example of how this strategy operates is shown in the way one school tackled the question of how to use tutorial time more effectively.

The first stage was the setting-up of a working party under the leadership of a house head to gather information about topics that teachers, pupils and parents thought ought to be covered, and then to check how far teachers believed these were covered in the existing subjects being taught in the school. This was a large task and, even using sampling, it took a year to provide an information base. However, this process of asking questions and collecting information brought home to everybody the lack of understood structure with regard to tutorial time.

Next, a staff conference was held to open up the question and to hear about approaches used by other schools. Douglas Hamblin was also invited to outline the study skills programme that he had developed (Hamblin 1981). It was made clear by giving information about various approaches that there was no simple solution, but at the same time people became increasingly aware of the need to do something.

The third stage in the process was in harnessing this awareness and forming working groups under the leadership of a deputy head.

A pastoral team working group defined areas in which materials and guidance were required and task groups of volunteers took up the areas in which they were interested. Individual interest was also encouraged and the main working group received suggestions for topics and for ways in which they might be presented. These were then given to other members of staff for review and refinement. This created a ripple effect as the interest of people on the edge of the initial groups was engaged by asking them to consider a suggestion and report their perception of the need for time on a particular topic.

At the same time as this was taking place there was a request from staff for help over specific counselling skills. This was met by arranging a staff conference with a county adviser followed by a series of follow-up meetings after school. These latter were voluntary but the attendance was high and the interest and involvement apparent. This provision of in-service training in response to need is effective and productive. A number of members of staff have gone on courses relating to the development of counselling skills and they will feed back their ideas.

However, the initial involvement of the whole staff in the activity at the staff conference has given the group as a whole a common experience relevant to a need that was seen to exist by all. The process is continuing, and it is necessary to ensure that all members of staff are kept informed of the developments and that momentum is maintained. The deputy involved in leading the working party

---

Pastoral Curriculum Working Party

Developments since last meeting:

I   *Methodology*
   (a) Hazel Johns – 3 sessions
       (1) Thursday, 2nd February, 4 p.m. Room 61
           Role play and simulation.
       (2) (Date to be arranged), 4 p.m. Room 61
           Tutor skills involved in running pastoral sessions
       (3) Thursday, 22nd March, 4 p.m. Room 61
           Counselling.
       The counselling session of the 22nd March will be followed by a series of meetings taken by members of Henbury Staff using the tapes on counselling (which are newly acquired, and can be borrowed from Isobel Shailes).
   (b) Isobel Shailes and Bob French are liaising with Hazel Johns and Jill Baldwin, Project Director of the *Active Tutorial Method*, to arrange a training course in Avon. This will, hopefully, take place in the autumn term; the training team is very busy so it could actually be later than this.
   (c) Isobel Shailes liaising with Liz Clarke, Training Manager of the *Lifeskills Teaching Programme*, with a view to arranging a one-day training session on *Teaching Lifeskills*.

II *Materials*
  (a) On order through librarian:
      EGAN, Gerard.
      The Skilled Helper – a Model for Systematic helping and
      Interpersonal Relating.
      You and Me: the skills of communicating and relating to others.
      ROGERS, Carl.
      On Becoming a Person.
  (b) On order through Bursar – will be available from Isobel's office:
       (i) Lifeskills Teaching Programme 2, and
      (ii) Teaching Lifeskills – Hopson and Scally.
  (c) Newly acquired – on loan:
      Active Tutorial 16–19.
      Tacade 'Free to Choose'. An approach to Drug Education.
      (Anne Miller intends to produce a unit on this topic.)
  (d) Phil Keeley, Graham Cartwright and Anne Miller are intending
      to produce a unit on 'Money Management'.
  (e) Sue Jobling and Isobel are working this term with the Open
      University, helping to prepare a unit on the Family, which will
      have a multi-disciplinary approach. We will be testing this unit
      in the school and it has been devised with a view to including it in
      our pastoral programme.
  (f) Isobel is in the process of asking certain members of staff to
      evaluate/review units on the following topics:
          Time management
          Life transitions
          Being positive about oneself
          Communicating effectively
          How to be assertive
          How to make, keep and end relationships
          How to manage negative emotions
          How to find a job.
      Other topics to be evaluated/reviewed, when preparation is
      completed:
          How to cope with stress
          How to study
          How to manage conflict
          How to give and receive feedback
          How to cope with unemployment
          How to work in groups.
      Opinions on suitability of the material will be fed back to the
      Working Party.

III Paul Wisbey is now representing us at the NAPCE (National
    Association for Pastoral Care in Education) Meetings at Bishopston
    Teachers' Centre and will inform us of speakers, materials, etc., that
    may be of value to the Working Party.

                                                        Isobel Shailes,
                                                        Deputy Head

Figure 6.2

reviews the rolling programme regularly and the involvement of many people is highlighted as is shown by a report sent to all members of staff (Figure 6.2).

The evaluation of the process will centre on the better use of tutorial time and the real judges of this will be the tutors themselves. Maurice Holt (1981, p. 157) has argued persuasively that parents are interested in 'the attitudes of staff, both as individuals and as reflecting the school's rationale of the curriculum'. Such an evaluation is a matter of defined educational stance and fits well with the approach of professional development as a vital part of the whole school organization.

I have developed a model from one produced in *School Organisation* (Lusty 1983, p. 376). This model illustrates the manner in which staff appraisal can be used in a formative manner to generate school development (see Figure 6.3). The follow-up, evaluation, planning for organizational development and review stages are best carried out by a small committee chaired by a coordinator. Such a coordinator will play a key part in the process and should be at deputy level within the school.

There are dangers in adopting the developmental strategy and it would be foolish to disregard these. On any map of new territory that is being explored there will be some areas marked 'Here be dragons'! First, there will be pressure on a school to streamline any policy for staff development so that it is easy to show that there is

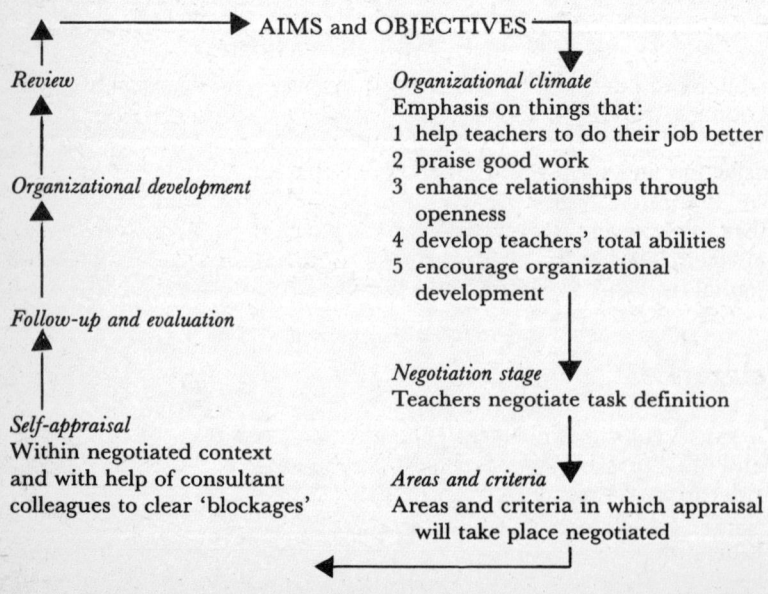

Figure 6.3

regular appraisal of staff. The purpose of this appraisal is not made clear and even when weaknesses are clearly identified nothing constructive is done. Secondly, schools can turn in on themselves and concentrate on developing their own procedures with scant regard to outside factors. This sort of parochialism can stunt real development. Thirdly, senior staff may lack the capacity or the courage to open up the procedures of running the school. Imagination and sensitivity are needed and there are expectations of a head of a school that he/she should direct the enterprise. A school-based staff development policy has to be initiated by leaders who know themselves and who believe in what they are doing. Fourthly, it is important to ensure that the structure of the organization is made clear and is understood. There is no greater frustration than that generated by role uncertainty. Finally, good communication and careful analysis of situations are vital. The head of a school must be frank and keep people informed. Criticism there must be, but if it is not constructive and made in terms of 'benefit language', then the atmosphere will grow sour.

There is no simple set of procedures which will bring about school-based staff development. The part played by the head is vital and it may help if the head's role is given a perspective rather different from the unpopular, lonely and 'task-oriented' figure described by Frank Musgrove (1971). The perspective is that of being a good coach. The good coach passes on his knowledge and experience, sets realistic standards of performance and takes constructive steps to help people attain these standards. Such a person understands that the development of human resources is the key to the success of the enterprise. The best coaches link their task to the everyday problems of the job. They do not hand out answers to problems; they encourage people to analyse problems and consider their own solutions. Socrates used this technique and the good head will find satisfaction and success if he/she adopts such an approach. Without such an approach a staff development policy rooted in a school will wither. People cannot be ordered to develop by even the most benevolent of despots but they can be encouraged to realize their full potential by an enthusiastic and positive coach.

References

BOLAM, R. (1980) 'In-service education and training' in E. Hoyle and J. Megarry, *Professional Development of Teachers*. World Education Yearbook. Kogan Page.

———— (1982) *School-focussed In-service Training*. Heinemman Educational Books.

DES (1972) *Teacher Education and Training* (James Report). HMSO.

HAMBLIN, D. (1981) *Teaching Study Skills*. Oxford: Blackwell.

HELLER, J. (1962) *Catch-22*. Cape.

HOLT, M. (1981) *Evaluating the Evaluators*. Dunton Green: Hodder & Stoughton.

HOYLE, E. (1973) 'Staff development in education – the search for a strategy: a response', in S. Pratt, *Staff Development in Education*. British Educational Administration Society. Councils and Education Press.

JOHN, D. (1971) 'The delegation of responsibility in large schools', *HMA Review*, LXIX (210).

JOYCE, B. (1980) 'The ecology of professional development', in E. Hoyle and J. Megarry, *Professional Development of Teachers*. World Education Yearbook. Kogan Page.

KATZ, D. and KAHN, R. (1978) *The Social Psychology of Organizations*. Chichester: Wiley.

LIGHT, A. J. (1973) 'Staff development in education – the search for a strategy', in S. Pratt, *Staff Development in Education*. British Educational Administration Society. Councils and Education Press.

LUSTY, M. (1983) 'Staff appraisal in the education service', *School Organisation*, 3 (4).

MILES, M. B. (1965) 'Planned change and organisational health, figure and ground' in R. O. Carbon, *Change Processes in the Public Schools*.

MUSGROVE, M. (1971) *Patterns of Power and Authority in English Education*. Methuen.

OLDROYD, D., SMITH, K. and LEE, J. (1984), *School-based Staff Development Activities: a Handbook for Secondary Schools*. York: Longman.

OPEN UNIVERSITY (1981) *The Management of Staff*, block six, E.323 Management and the School. Milton Keynes: Open University Press.

TAYLOR, W. (1980) 'Professional development or personal development', in E. Hoyle and J. Megarry, *Professional Development of Teachers*. World Education Yearbook. Kogan Page.

7   Helping with Stress

Jack Dunham

Any responsibility post in a school is primarily concerned with facilitating the work of other adults. Most of the tasks described so far have not been concerned with the worries or strains of those other adults, and yet a teacher is likely to experience a variety of kinds of stress that are inherent in the profession. The management task must include helping those teachers cope with that stress. The responsibility holder, too, has additional stresses that come from work with other adults, often other teachers previously thought of as allies against difficult pupils, parents and the outside world. This kind of managerial stress often comes unexpectedly, and often goes deep and hurts. Teachers carrying responsibility are better able to cope with the stress in their managerial task if they can consciously work on it. Thus they have the double job of helping themselves and helping those for whom they are responsible. This chapter considers the classroom teacher's stress and ways of coping.

MM

The first step in tackling stress is to acknowledge its existence in teaching. Acceptance is difficult for people who associate stress with personal weakness and professional incompetence. For them, admitting to classroom difficulties is paramount to admitting that they are bad teachers. They are afraid to disclose professional problems to colleagues who would regard them as signs of failure. They are unwilling to ask for help because that action would be seen as a form of weakness. These barriers to stress reduction were reported by two teachers who were members of my in-service training courses in 1983. One comment was made by a head of department:

> The awareness of stress is an important issue. Many people seem unable to recognize the signs in themselves or feel that they are letting themselves down if they admit to stress.

More obstructive beliefs were identified by a teacher in a school for maladjusted children:

> Pressure is built into the job and I am well supported but I am also subject to pride which at moments of most need tells me, falsely, that to seek help is to show weakness and that if I can't stand the heat I shouldn't be in the kitchen.

The second step is to be clear about what the term 'stress' means because several definitions are used by teachers. This issue of meaning is important because we need to know which definition teachers are using when they accept or deny the existence of stress.

There are three major approaches to understanding stress. The first approach looks at the pressures exerted on teachers in schools. They are exposed to demands from many sources which may arise from the job itself, from the environment in which they work and from their relationships with their colleagues. The second approach is concerned with teachers' reactions to these pressures, which may include learning new techniques and skills, but which may also consist of emotional and bodily reactions such as headaches and muscular tension. A major concern is whether long-term organizational stress can lead to more serious reactions such as exhaustion and breakdown. The third approach attempts to understand stress in terms of the interaction between teachers and the school organization. It is closely involved in identifying the pressures and reactions which teachers define as stressful, and attention is directed to the coping behaviour teachers use as they attempt to reduce or prevent stress.

This interactionist perspective is helpful in suggesting possible answers to the question of why there are marked individual differences in teachers' reactions to the same experience, for example, reorganization. Some teachers who were involved in the transition from small grammar schools, in which curriculum and other changes were infrequent, to large comprehensive schools, where they were confronted by many changes, managed the adjustment without suffering psychosomatic reactions or anxiety or frustrations, while colleagues engaged in the same process became irritable, could not sleep and felt depressed. In this process of adaptation what determines a teacher's 'tolerance for stress' and his/her 'capacity for adaptation'? Under the circumstances of organizational and curricular changes within schools why do some teachers fairly rapidly begin to develop stress symptoms while others show signs of a marked immunity to these demands and some respond by an increased zest in their teaching?

The answers to these questions are of considerable significance in any discussion about helping teachers to cope with organizational stress. The interactionist view is that the extent to which a teacher experiences stress in any situation depends first on the manner in which the task requirements and the abilities to deal with them are assessed. Secondly, it depends on how the individual anticipates likely future demanding experiences and his/her readiness to cope with them. Thirdly, the experience of stress is determined by the extent of the preparation and rehearsal of the skills necessary for the teacher to handle pressures effectively. An important part of preparation is awareness and the next section is concerned with the major pressures which teachers have identified.

Sources of stress

In studies of stress in schools teachers have identified many pressures. In one investigation by Kyriacou and Sutcliffe (1977), teachers in comprehensive schools were asked to rate each of 51 sources of stress in response to the question: 'As a teacher, how great a source of stress are these factors to you?' Their answers to this question indicated four major sources of stress:
1 Pupil misbehaviour: noisy pupils, difficult classes, difficult behaviour problems
2 Poor working conditions: poor career structure, poor promotion opportunities, inadequate salary, shortage of equipment
3 Time pressures: not enough time to do the work and too much work to do
4 Poor school ethos: inadequate disciplinary policy at school, lack of consensus on minimum standards, and the behaviour of the headteacher.

The results of this investigation are similar to those produced in my studies of teachers in primary and secondary schools (Dunham 1976, 1980), but there are important differences to be noted. My research indicates that four major areas of concern have been reported by teachers:
1 Educational change: reorganization and too many innovations in the curriculum and in teaching methods
2 Problem pupils: lack of interest, inattention, apathy, lack of effort and concentration, hostility, lack of cooperation, disruption
3 Poor working conditions: large size schools and classes and high noise levels, poor staff communication and cooperation
4 Role conflict and role confusion: an increasing number of expectations placed on teachers.

Reorganization has not been a source of stress for all the teachers who have experienced it. For some members of staff it has brought opportunities for fresh patterns of teaching, new relationships, involvement in exciting curricular developments, better prospects for promotion and for personal and professional growth. But other teachers have had severe adjustment problems which had five major aspects:

1 Leaving the security of a known environment
2 Working in a large(r) organization
3 Teaching children who have a much wider range of abilities, attitudes and behaviour
4 Major organizational changes
5 Major curricular changes.

These reorganization pressures were concerned with expansion but for most teachers its current meaning is associated with the contraction of the education service. An indication of some of the pressures which this development has produced can be seen in the following excerpt from a letter sent to me by the head of a secondary school inviting me to take part in an in-service training day:

> This school is a three-form entry girls' secondary modern school. At present the roll stands at 500 but this will soon drop to approximately 465. There are 30 members of staff including myself. I believe that my staff, in common with those in other schools, are under considerable pressure at the moment with falling rolls and the prospect of re-organization of the city schools in a year's time. I shall be grateful if you can air this problem and give us some guidance in coping with it as a staff.

Reorganization, whether old style or new style, has had the additional complication of major problems of role conflict and role uncertainty. I have investigated these pressures by adapting for use in educational research and training a check-list which was originally prepared for industrial research (Kahn 1973).

I have used this check-list frequently in my work with teachers, and information from these small surveys is given in Table 7.1. The first column gives data from a local education authority conference on stress when I was one of the contributors. The other results refer to single-school staff conferences when I was the tutor for an in-service training day.

The numbers involved in these recent investigations are small but the pattern set by these results is sufficiently consistent to support the conclusion that role conflict and role ambiguity have increased in secondary schools.

Two types of role conflict can be identified from teachers' reports of their pressures. The first arises because of contradictory expectations as, for example, in the role of deputy head who may be seen by the head as a member of the top management team and by staff as the link between the staffroom and the 'top corridor'.

It also occurs for headteachers when parental expectations of pupil achievement, behaviour and attitudes are in conflict with staff expectations and the head becomes the fulcrum for these opposing pressures, doing a precarious balancing act in the middle of them.

Heads of department may experience this kind of role conflict when they act as intermediaries between their own department and other departments in the school or with the heads of houses and years. The head of department is also the link between the teachers in his department and the headteacher. The former may perceive his function to be to put their point of view to the head, while the latter may perceive the head of department's role to have an important controlling function.

These conflicting demands also make a significant contribution to the work pressures of the pastoral heads. They are often presented with disciplinary and pastoral problems which require their attention when they have urgent teaching duties or which require them to be the mediator between pupils, parents and colleagues.

These demands originating from different sources are important causes of one kind of role conflict. But another type can also be identified. This occurs because management posts in school contain several parts of other people's roles. These include counsellor,

Table 7.1   Percentage of teachers identifying certain stress situations

	LEA Conference – all types of schools 300 teachers 1977	Comprehensive schools		
		A 43 staff 1982	B 28 staff 1983	C 58 staff 1983
1 Felt that you had too little authority to carry out your responsibilities?	13	20	24	22
2 Felt unclear what the scope and responsibilities of your job were?	12	37	21	29
3 Felt that you had too heavy a work-load?	18	46	78	68
4 Thought that you were not able to satisfy the conflicting demands of your colleagues, parents of your pupils, pupils, etc.?	15	38	57	50
5 Did not know how your head/head of department/pastoral team leader evaluated your teaching and tutorial work?	28	32	32	24
6 Found yourself unable to get the information needed to carry out your job?	8	23	10	18
7 Felt unable to influence the LEA's decisions and actions that affected you?	18	23	32	49
8 Did not know what the people you worked with expected of you?	5	20	10	13
9 Thought that the amount of work you had to do interfered with how well it was done?	30	69	82	82
10 Felt that you had to do things at school that were against your better judgement?	23	60	42	29

careers adviser, social worker, teacher, manager, resource provider, examiner, secretary, restaurant manager, librarian and education adviser.

The third major source of stress identified by teachers is the behaviour of disruptive pupils. The term is subject to different interpretations and a report by Clwyd County Council (1976) lists the following elements of disruptive behaviour in order of frequency of occurrence: rowdyism, actual violence, damage to property, threats of violence, theft and sexual misbehaviour. The incidence of rowdyism (characterized by 'deliberate lateness to lessons, disturbance in the lessons, verbal abuse and refusal to co-operate') in one week was reported as eighty-four incidents per thousand pupils and actual violence and damage to property was put at ten incidents per thousand pupils. The expression of pupil anger can be a disturbing and frightening experience for teachers whose personal values and previous experience have led them to believe that the right way to deal with angry feelings is to control them tightly and to hide them from other people.

Another factor in teaching 'problem' pupils is concerned with difficulties in staff relationships. The report of a head of house in a staff conference which I organized indicates this complication as a major source of stress:

> In my position as Head of House I have to try and balance the pupils' interest against the staff and the philosophy of the school. This has led to confrontations with junior staff, senior staff and finally the Head. In one instance the staff found the pupil's antics to be highly amusing, e.g. pretending to be a 'dead fly' during art lessons. However, when indiscipline crept in then the staff gave up and wanted me to deal with it. Parental support for the boy was negligible. The final conflict was a head-on clash with the Head over the pupil's suspension resulting in disciplinary action against myself being threatened. The pupil was suspended on many occasions and put into a unit for disruptive pupils. I felt that I was always fighting a losing battle against the staff who were not interested in the boy's long-term problems.

These major problems of reorganization, role-conflict and teaching disruptive pupils are exacerbated by another source of stress which has been identified by teachers as 'poor working conditions'. There are three important aspects of this problem; physical, social and financial.

The physical aspects of poor working conditions include old buildings, poorly constructed buildings, noisy conditions caused by inadequate insulation and soundproofing, open-plan design, loud bells, and external traffic noise. Cox (1977) also cites as possible causes of stress: overcrowding, poor quality buildings, old buildings, and split-site schools with their difficulties of commuting between buildings.

Little attention has been paid to the effects of noise in schools, even though research in industry has established that noise can impair hearing, lead to changes in physiological balance and be responsible for psychological effects which include poor concentration, fatigue and sudden changes of mood (Eysenck 1975). Carlestam (1971) maintains that noise, which he describes as 'unwanted sound', is one of the environmental factors that has a great impact on people. The disturbing effect of noise on humans is due to several factors, the most important being loudness, composition and duration. When the decibel count exceeds 90, the sense of hearing is physiologically affected, gradually leading to chronic deafness. Carlestam also points out that noise levels of lower intensity can also harm the individual and give rise to mental and psychosomatic effects.

The social aspects of poor working conditions include difficult and frustrating staff relationships and poor communications which may result in little support by top management of junior teachers, poor cooperation between the academic and pastoral concerns, and conflict between the departments. One major consequence of poor communications is a lack of support by colleagues of teachers with professional problems.

The financial aspects of poor working conditions appear to be increasingly significant. Reduced school budgets have meant lower levels of expenditure on equipment and textbooks. Smaller LEA funds have resulted in the redeployment of teachers and will lead to further redundancies and school closures.

The financial aspects of poor working conditions have important 'fall-out' effects on the physical and organizational conditions in school. The effects can be recognized in the deterioration in the maintenance and repair functions but they have been felt most directly in the classroom. The lack of money for school resources has hampered the development of new courses and blocked the use of up-dated textbooks.

Another important consequence of contraction is a radical change in career expectations. Many teachers entered the profession with a vertical model of achievement based on promotion. In the early part of their careers this model was not unrealistic: they were promoted to middle-management posts in their late twenties or early thirties with the strong assumption that further progress would follow. These assumptions must now be re-examined. It is often a painful process because these are new kinds of problems to people whose previous work experience has been spent in a period of expansion.

Reactions to pressures

Staff reactions to these pressures can be grouped into four main categories: behavioural, emotional, mental and physical. These reactions can also be placed in a framework of successive stages which staff pass through as their work (and home) pressures become increasingly severe. First, they develop new coping techniques or continue to use familiar strategies. If these coping actions are unsuccessful in reducing pressures, a number of emotional and mental reactions are experienced. These include frustration, anger, anxiety, fear, poor concentration and memory loss. Severe physical reactions occur when exposure to stress is prolonged. These include heart attacks, ulcers and skin disorders. Continued exposure to the stress situations identified earlier in the chapter, without a corresponding increase in coping resources, brings fatigue, exhaustion and burn-out.

This framework is based on three theoretical perspectives which I have found helpful in understanding teachers' reactions to stress. The first theory identified three stages: the alarm reaction, the stage of resistance and the state of exhaustion. The alarm is invoked when the individual becomes aware of a stress situation. At this stage increased hormone secretions, including adrenalin, enter the blood-stream to help him/her cope with the increased demands. If the demands are not reduced, the physiological responses, which may include changes in the heart rate and pulse rate as well as hormone secretions, are maintained at a higher level than normal for the individual in order to resist increasing demands. This strains and drains the body's resources. This could lead, for example, to a marked loss in body weight. Finally, if the stress continues, the body continues to draw on its deeper level of resources in a desperate attempt to cope. Exhaustion may be experienced at this stage, while prolonged exposure to severe stress may result in death (Selye 1974).

The second theoretical perspective which is helpful in under-standing stress reactions has been proposed by Appley and Trumbull (1967), who suggest that individuals pass through stress thresholds as they respond to increasing pressures. The first level consists of changes in behaviour which are used by the individual in an attempt to cope with new or increased demands. Appley and Trumbull call this the 'new coping behaviour threshold'. At this stage dissatisfaction can be prevented from degenerating into stress in that changes are sought which will remedy, at least partially, an unsatisfactory situation. If these attempts are unsuccessful in coping with the situation, the 'frustration threshold' is reached. If there is a continuing failure to cope, an individual may begin to question his/her competence and will experience strong feelings of anxiety. More severe disturbances may lead to the development of psycho-somatic symptoms. As the individual uses up his/her coping resources he/she will reach and pass through the threshold of exhaustion.

The third theory looks at the relationship between the performance of the teacher's role and the demands which are

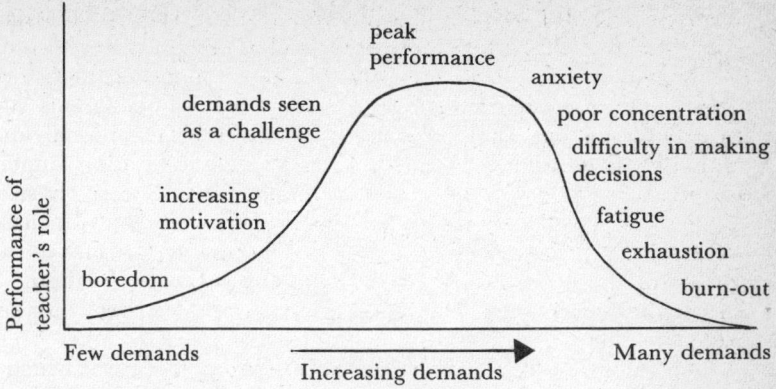

Figure 7.1

experienced. This relationship is expressed in Figure 7.1. In this theory Hebb (1972) has proposed that work with only few demands leads to boredom. Increasing demands are regarded as stimulating and energizing, but if they are beyond the person's coping abilities they lead to high levels of anxiety and reduced effectiveness in the job. Continued demands without an increase in coping resources may lead to fatigue, exhaustion and burn-out.

These reactions have been reported by teachers in studies of stress in schools (Kyriacou 1981, Dunham 1976, 1980). My recent research has involved the use of a check-list in three comprehensive schools which had invited me to lead their staff development conferences in 1982 and 1983. The teachers were asked to indicate which reactions they had experienced in the present school year, and a rough assessment of their frequency was sought by asking them to identify which they had experienced Very Often, Often, Sometimes and Rarely. The information from these surveys given in Table 7.2 is restricted to the percentage of teachers who identified each reaction Very Often or Often.

The 'Any other' item identified several reactions which were not included in my check-list. These were feelings of tearfulness, need for increased sleep, loss of self-confidence, palpitations, asthma, muscular pains in shoulders, worry, indigestion, erratic work habits, restlessness, resentment, disappointment, lethargy, fear of failure, loss of sex drive, high blood pressure, deterioration in self-esteem and feeling numb.

These behavioural, mental, emotional and physical signs of stress show a wide range of reactions to occupational pressures. It is therefore important to offset this perspective by noting that some teachers have reported that they can handle heavy demands in school without experiencing any of these stress reactions. If their coping strategies can be identified and then shared with colleagues

Table 7.2   Percentage of staff in three English comprehensive schools identifying stress reactions

	Comprehensive schools		
	A	B	C
1 Large increase in consumption of alcohol	0	10	3
2 Marital or family conflict	3	5	14
3 The marked reduction of contacts with people outside school	36	22	35
4 Displaced aggression – displacement on to children or people outside school	20	18	14
5 Apathy	25	18	14
6 Wanting to leave teaching	25	15	20
7 Unwilling to support colleagues	0	0	3
8 Strong feelings of being unable to cope	7	16	8
9 Irritability	18	34	24
10 Moodiness	7	19	22
11 The inability to make decisions	0	4	6
12 Feverish activity with little purpose	7	18	10
13 Inability to concentrate	14	8	10
14 Absenteeism	0	0	3
15 Depression	3	11	8
16 Tension headaches	14	15	18
17 Feelings of exhaustion	36	46	41
18 Frustration because there was little sense of achievement	32	30	16
19 Withdrawal from staff contact	14	7	14
20 Anger	7	11	12
21 Anxiety	3	23	16
22 Loss of sleep	14	15	14
23 Loss of weight	0	5	0
24 Feelings of isolation in school	10	8	11
25 Feelings of fear	0	8	3
26 Feelings of guilt	7	10	9
27 Over-eating	14	15	14
28 Skin rash	3	5	0
29 Large increase in smoking	0	4	9
30 Hyper-sensitivity to criticism	7	11	18
31 Back pain	7	8	7
32 Any other			

suffering from stress a good start will have been made towards stress reduction and prevention. The next section is therefore concerned with the resources which teachers use to reduce stress.

Teachers' coping resources

My research has revealed considerable differences between teachers in their responses to similar experiences in school – for example, some teachers identified few signs of adverse reactions during reorganization while others gave several indications of positive responses such as an increased zest in their teaching. These results directed my attention to the strategies teachers use when they encounter heavy work pressures. I found that they were using a broad range of skills, techniques, knowledge, experience, relationships and activities which I collectively term 'resources' and which I classify into four categories: personal, interpersonal, organizational and community.

My attempts to identify the resources which staff were using to reduce stress were based on two methods. I asked them 'How do you try to reduce your work stress?' and I also invited them to identify their coping strategies on a check-list. Their answers to this question and the items that were ticked on the check-list can be grouped into my suggested four categories.

Personal resources included work strategies, positive attitudes and out-of-school activities. Direct attempts to cope alone with stress in school included switching-off, trying to come to terms with each individual situation, self-pacing, keeping work and home as separate as possible, bringing feelings and opinions out into the open, acceptance of the problem and learning the job in more detail. The out-of-school activities which teachers used as individuals to reduce feelings of tension, anger and agitation included gardening, painting, walking, cooking, baking, cycling, driving their cars fast, and praying.

The interpersonal resources which teachers used included talking over stressful incidents with spouse or family, meeting people who were unconnected with teaching, and talking to a friend who had a similar job and using him or her as a sounding board and 'verbal punching bag'.

Organizational resources came from good relationships in school when they were able to discuss their problems, worries and feelings with their colleagues. They also included supportive departmental, pastoral and senior management teams, in-service and induction courses for probationers and other staff, and help from advisers and education officers.

Community activities reported by teachers included bell ringing, squash, badminton, football, drama, chess clubs, and choral singing. Some reports indicate an importance for these activities beyond that of relaxation or pleasure. They seem to have enabled staff to assume life styles which were alternatives to those followed in their professional roles.

Some of the coping methods used by teachers are indicated in the following brief reports:

Personal resources

Work strategies
By working harder – this certainly raises my self-esteem and not infrequently removes the cause of a stressful situation.

Making a positive effort to be more efficient and organized.

By clearer planning of what has to be done with specific time allocations.

Positive attitudes
Recognizing the dangers of allowing stress factors to combine in my mind so that I reach hyper-self-critical conclusions: I'm under stress; I can't cope; I can't teach; I'm an inadequate person.

Attempting to encourage within myself a more confident attitude towards the job.

Try not to worry about other people's jobs – do your own well and leave others to answer for their decisions.

Out-of-school activities
Hard physical exercise.

Meditation, relaxation techniques and yoga exercises.

Writing – either letters to friends or relations or short stories sometimes based on personal stress.

Interpersonal resources

I reduce my stress by talking things through with my husband who isn't in the profession.

My supportive relationship with my wife is of enormous help, not just providing overt and tacit reassurance but also because of the physical benefits of a loving and satisfying sexual life.

I am not afraid of discussing my problems with, or relating my 'horrific' days to, a friend outside school.

Organizational resources

Your course was stimulating, useful and practical. Of course the practice is quite hard and I certainly felt a 'low' on Monday when the daily grind with all its pressures reasserted itself. However, I have notes to look back on and I am 'forcing' myself to keep these on top of the desk. I will be giving a report to the head later this week and I hope to disseminate the ideas to the staff development group soon.

I have very good relationships with colleagues, especially with my immediate most senior colleagues, which facilitate and make more effective our mutual support.

I have a few colleagues with whom (in different areas of work) it is possible to let off steam and explode in frustration.

Community resources

I reduce pressure in myself by getting involved in outside activities which have nothing to do with teaching and by rarely seeing friends amongst the staff out of school. I suspect the reason I don't arrange social meetings is because deep down I want to forget about work when I'm away from it.

Table 7.3   Percentage of staff in three English comprehensive schools identifying coping resources

Coping resources	Comprehensive schools		
	A	B	C
How have you reduced your work stress this school year? (Asterisks indicate the ten most frequently used coping strategies.)			
1 By learning my job in more detail	27	14	31
2 By not going to school	0	2	2
3 * Tried to come to terms with each individual situation	50	50	48
4 * Acceptance of the problem	72	35	41
5 * By talking over stressful situations with my husband/wife/family	50	46	48
6 * By switching off	50	44	43
7 Going on a course	17	2	9
8 By moving away from the situation completely for a time until the stress had been reduced	22	12	14
9 * Trying to bring my feelings and opinions into the open	50	44	41
10 When away from work trying to make sure that I had a good time wherever I went	22	35	29
11 * By involving myself with my family and my own circle of friends when I was not working	47	55	39
12 Trying to think that I was only human and can make mistakes	47	42	29
13 Shutting myself in my office	11	2	0
14 Meeting people who were totally unconnected with teaching	27	33	31
15 I tended to blot out work when I got home and refused to talk about it	5	21	9
16 I tried to get out as much as possible on the weekend – going for walks, to the museum, to see a film	17	31	7
17 Forcing myself to take rests before getting tired	22	14	9
18 * By talking about it, usually with colleagues at school	27	50	41
19 * Trying to say 'No' to unnecessary demands	50	55	33
20 * I now admit my limits more easily than when I first became a teacher	27	50	43
21 At home I tried to relax by doing something which gives a simple sense of achievement and success, e.g. baking, knitting, gardening, etc.	33	34	33
22 * By setting aside a certain amount of time during the evenings and at weekends during which I refused to do anything at all connected with school	55	76	53
23 Any other(s)			

These brief reports of coping strategies can now be compared with my second method of investigation which was the use of a resources check-list. The results of this method can be seen in Table 7.3.

The 'Any other' item on the check-list enabled me to compile a list of additional resources which included jogging, becoming more detached, listening to music, talking to deputy and head, swimming, going out and getting drunk, taking the pressure off by playing squash, making love, seeking promotion elsewhere, learning greater self-control, and grumbling a lot.

The results of my research are quite similar to the coping actions identified in a study of staff stress in secondary schools reported by Kyriacou (1981). In his investigation three different types of resources were used. The first consisted of talking about problems and feelings with other people and seeking support from friends, colleagues and family. The second kind focused on different ways of dealing with the sources of stress. The third type of coping actions was mainly directed towards out-of-school activities which seemed to be aimed at distracting the teachers' attention away from stress at work to more pleasurable and relaxing interests.

Kyriacou also asked the teachers which strategies they most often used to try to reduce stress. The twenty most frequently used coping actions were:

1 Try to keep things in perspective
2 Try to avoid confrontations
3 Try to relax after work
4 Try to take some immediate action on the basis of your present understanding of the situation
5 Think objectively about the situation and keep your feelings under control
6 Stand back and rationalize the situation
7 Try to nip potential sources of stress in the bud
8 Try to reassure yourself everything is going to work out all right
9 Do not let the problem go until you have solved it or reconciled it satisfactorily
10 Make sure people are aware you are doing your best
11 Try to forget work when the day is finished
12 Try to see the humour of the situation
13 Consider a range of plans for handling the sources of stress – set priorities
14 Make a concerted effort to enjoy yourself with some pleasurable activity after work
15 Try not to worry or think about it
16 Express your feelings and frustrations to others so that you can think rationally about the problem
17 Throw yourself into work and work harder and longer
18 Think of good things in the future
19 Talk about the situation with someone at work
20 Express your irritation to colleagues at work just to be able to let off steam.

This list of teachers' coping methods identified by Kyriacou's research and the information from my investigations provide a sound basis for anyone wanting to learn to cope with stress more effectively. But it is possible to add to this store and the next section is concerned with methods of augmenting personal strategies.

Strengthening personal resources

Much has been written about how to cope more effectively with stress. Panaceas are authoritatively recommended and relaxation, diet, jogging and bio-feedback have been proposed as the definitive cure. Lists of recommended coping actions have also been published. Typical of these schedules is a nine-point plan compiled by Masidlover (1981):

1 Take time to relax
2 Talk about your problems
3 Plan your tasks so you can easily handle them
4 Deal with your anger
5 Get away for a while
6 Be realistic in your goals
7 Avoid self-medication
8 Learn to accept what you can't change
9 Look after your body.

One major problem with these packages of advice is that there is no suggested framework which can be used for the integration of recommendations into a coherent, individualized stress-reduction programme. In my work with teachers in conferences, courses and counselling I use the following framework.

Guidelines for learning how to reduce stress
1 The first step is to accept that you are having pressures and reactions which you are not coping with effectively
2 The second step is to decide that your coping resources can be strengthened
3 You will probably find it helpful to identify your pressures and reactions as separate problems which need to be tackled separately in your stress-reduction programme
4 Your stress-reduction training will enable you to develop a wide range of personal, interpersonal, organizational and community resources which you can use to deal with your pressures and reactions
5 Your stress-reduction programme has three phases:
   (a) *Education* – so you can develop a conceptual framework to understand your pressures, reactions and resources
   (b) *Rehearsal and application* – in which you can learn to use the appropriate coping skills and other resources
   (c) *Feedback and review* – to evaluate the coping skills which are being used to reduce stress.

The first guideline – acceptance of stress – is the platform for the successful accomplishment of all the other stages. The first step requires you to challenge and if necessary change some beliefs about your job which you may have held very strongly for a number of years, including the following:

1 My job is my life and my life is my job.
2 In my position I must be totally competent, knowledgeable and able to help all the staff (or children). I must always work at my peak level with a lot of energy and enthusiasm.
3 To be able to accomplish my job and for my self-esteem I must be liked and respected by everyone I work with.
4 Getting any form of negative feedback about my work indicates that there is something wrong in what I am doing.
5 Things must work out the way I want them to.

The fifth guideline recommends the development of a stress-reduction programme the first phase of which – educational – enables a teacher to learn the concepts and language which are needed to understand the connection between pressures and reactions and the importance of coping resources. The second phase – rehearsal and application – involves learning new skills and also self-coping statements which are used whenever the teacher feels threatened by stress. These statements are concerned with the four aspects of coping. These are: preparing for a major pressure, handling the stress situation, tackling disturbing and frightening reactions in yourself, giving self-congratulation for having coped. Examples of these self-coping statements are:

Preparing for a major pressure – What is it I have to do? I can develop a plan to deal with it.

Handling the stress situation – I can handle the situation one step at a time. It is normal to feel anxious now.

Tackling disturbing and frightening reactions – I knew that my anxiety would rise. It will all be finished soon. It is not the worst thing that can happen.

Self-congratulatory statements – I was able to do it. I made more of the situation than it was worth.

This phase of the programme also includes learning to use skills and one of the most important will possibly be relaxation. Few of the teachers I work with have taken a course in relaxation training. There are several different methods available – some starting at the feet and working upwards and some working downwards from the scalp. I use different approaches in my stress-reduction training courses. The shortest exercise is:

Two minutes relaxation skill
Breathe evenly and calmly
Think about relaxing your body
Think about the tension draining from your feet, legs, body, arms, neck and shoulders

Notice the tension draining from your body.

The third phase of the programme is the evaluation of these new skills in reducing stress. Several review techniques can be used including comparing the stress reaction check-list profile at the beginning of the programme and at intervals of about six months.

These methods for strengthening personal resources might appear to be merely palliative to those teachers who want 'direct action' recommendations to help them develop school-based strategies and actions. The next section is therefore concerned with increasing organizational support.

Strengthening organizational resources

Teachers have made many recommendations for strengthening organizational resources but their main proposals were: effective selection procedures, induction programmes for all staff, the expansion of staff development opportunities and more support from colleagues and LEA staff.

The improvement of staff selection, which is increasingly important in a time of contraction, can be achieved by following a systematic process in which there are three essential requirements:
1 Interviewers should know what they are assessing in the candidates by preparing a job description
2 Interviewers should know how to assess the key factors in the candidates by the use of a systematic interview
3 Interviewers should be aware of the importance of regularly reviewing the effectiveness of their selection procedures.

The effectiveness of the selection procedures can be assessed by reviewing the adjustment and progress of the person appointed. The first appraisal interview should take place not more than three months after the appointment and should be regarded as a vital part of the school's induction programme. This link is important and if it is weak the advantages of improvements in the selection process may be lost. Strong induction programmes should be regarded as key organizational resources.

There should be a structured schedule of training for probationers paying particular attention to the unexpected pressures they are experiencing, their reactions to these demands and their coping strategies. My investigation of these demands for which the probationers were not prepared by their training courses suggests that they include the following shocks: spending so much time commuting between the sites of the school; teaching classes of remedial children; having many forms to complete; having to do a half-term assessment on every pupil in their classes; the indiscipline of the pupils; being a first-year tutor; having large groups of mixed

CSE/O-level pupils; different attitudes and ideals among staff largely due to age differences; losing free periods to cover for absent colleagues; high noise levels which make you want to scream; having a head who wanders round the school and peers through the class-room windows.

There is also a strong need for an induction programme for newcomers to the school who are not probationers. It should include a letter of introduction and welcome from the appropriate member of the middle-management or senior-management teams and participation in groupwork sessions in which the course members can share their growing understanding of the school's aims, organizational structure and systems. It should also include the first of the regular interviews with a senior member of staff which will be the introduction to a systematic staff appraisal schedule. These regular reviews provide good opportunities for the satisfaction of important teachers' needs which include knowing what is expected of them; having feedback about how their work is evaluated; being able to discuss their difficulties objectively and constructively; feeling valued by receiving recognition for effort as well as achievement; being aware of personal and professional growth.

It is a good organizational resource when the appraisal system is linked to the in-service training provision so that appropriate opportunities are offered for continuing staff development. This linking is particularly significant for those members of staff who because of contraction of promotion opportunities are now feeling 'trapped' in their present posts and are frightened that their job prospects may not improve. These career development problems need urgent attention and they were a major concern for the heads of departments and pastoral care heads on my management courses in 1983. Their specific questions were: 'What opportunities exist for staff at this level for horizontal movement say to teacher training, advisory work, or teacher centre management?'; 'How do we find out about and prepare for these opportunities?'; 'What are the prospects for re-entry into the education system if we take a job outside teaching?'

These men and women with middle-management responsibilities were very interested in preparing for promotion by improving their skills in writing letters of application and in being interviewed. They were less aware of the need to analyse carefully the knowledge and skills which are required for effective performance of the post they might apply for or the need to make a realistic appraisal of the pressures experienced by the post holder and the resources required to cope with them effectively.

But helping staff to prepare for non-promotion is also an important task of a staff development programme. The inclusion of this topic may appear negative and defeatist to some teachers but there are others who are relieved that this concern has been brought out into the open at last. This issue of the possibility of no further promotion is particularly painful for those teachers who have identified most strongly with the vertical model of personal and professional development. This model equates achievement with promotion and it appears to have been generally accepted in a time of expansion of the education service. In the present contraction it is less valid and a horizontal model of personal and professional growth might be more appropriate. This model offers many alternatives to promotion as sources of achievement, job satisfaction and new professional challenges. One alternative can be found in job rotation. An example of this approach is the periodic exchange of the deputy heads' responsibilities in a secondary school. Another possibility is exchange between establishments. Becoming involved in new developments in the curriculum, for instance in the pastoral programme, can bring further expansion to the range of teachers' work. I have good opportunities for observing these developments in my participation in the training of staff to teach Education in Personal Relationships courses in Gloucestershire secondary schools. These teachers have reported ten positive aspects of teaching these programmes:

1 It is an aid to revitalization and the removal of stagnation
2 It takes you out of your litte 'box' in the eyes of the children
3 There is more rapport with the children because you are showing a greater understanding of their problems and not just teaching a subject
4 The methods used to teach EPR can be carried over into your subject area
5 It is a change not to be on a set syllabus connected with exams
6 It allows greater self-awareness and self-development for pupils and teachers
7 EPR helps to create an open and caring ethos in school
8 Teachers can learn from pupils
9 It brings cross-curricular teaching which involves meeting new staff and learning new teaching techniques
10 It is enjoyable to teach because the material used is relevant to pupils.

This is a good example of the job enlargement schemes which have been used for a number of years in the management of industrial organizations (Cotgrove, Dunham and Vamplew 1971). They have recently started to appear in discussions of educational management as, for instance, in Bone (1983).

Staff development programmes should also be concerned with strengthening organizational resources by helping staff to develop their skills of communication, cooperation and social support. Considerable thought, time and effort should be given to the growth of strong teamwork to achieve and maintain caring departmental and pastoral teams. The team meeting is not the only medium by which these aims can be achieved but it is an influential one. Meetings should be consistently effective by means of good planning, clearly presented aims, good organization of the inter- action between members, well formulated decisions and actions, and follow-up procedures to check the effectiveness of the decisions. Management training to achieve these goals is now a realistic possibility for every school as there are books, materials and courses available to provide the impetus for INSET (Marland and Hill 1981).

The awareness of group behaviour which is stimulated by this kind of programme is an important stage in the creation of a team which is a source of social support for its members. But social support should not be restricted to colleagues in departments and houses or years. Many members of staff benefit from discussing their problems with an attentive listener. The major benefits are to be able to put stress situations into perspective which enables them to take corrective action, and also to receive reassurance that the diffi- culties have not been caused by serious personal and professional weaknesses. But staff care should not be limited to crisis management. These are positive aspects which should permeate all relationships in the school organization. This goal was expressed very clearly by the staff of an English secondary school which I used in my comparison of staff stress in English and German comprehen- sive schools (Dunham 1980). Their major recommendation was:

> It is very important for teachers to be told how well or not they are working and how valued or not are their ideas and contributions. Constructive criticism is essential provided it is constructive and not destructive. We all need from time to time assurance that we are on the right lines or alternatively sympathetic guiding on to those lines. I suppose if people care enough about what they are doing and enough about the people with whom they have to work then empathy is not difficult. We must have opportunities to express our anxieties and problems without fearing repercussions on our careers.

Many teachers seem to believe that it is the responsibility of senior management to initiate the support they need. This point of view has many adherents. One of them presented this proposition quite categorically:

> Much of the responsibility for improving the social support a teacher receives in school must inevitably rest with the Head . . . It is important that the Head should take the initiative by seeking to find out the problems facing his own senior staff . . . and showing himself to be receptive to their difficulties thereby setting an example which they would be expected to follow. (Kyriacou 1981, p. 59)

I disagree quite strongly with this belief for a number of reasons: first, because of the severe pressures on the senior management team; secondly, it implies a one-directional flow of support from the top downwards; and thirdly, because it reinforces the expectations of teachers that senior staff will tell them how to cope, which increases their vulnerability when support is not available.

My model is different in that it seeks to open up pathways of support in all directions in an organization – upwards, sideways and downwards. It encourages the sharing of resources between all members of the school community – teachers, non-teaching staff and pupils. It proposes an active policy of participation by all members in the continuing development of a school as a healthy organization (Gardell 1971).

Each school should establish its own stress-reduction programmes which should include projects by departmental and pastoral teams. One project was initiated by a head of department after taking part in one of my stress workshops. She wrote an evaluation six months later for the follow-up session:

Attempts to reduce pressure
I have tried quite hard to do something positive here.

1 Departmental – we continue to hold weekly departmental meetings in order to allow views to be shared as well as for the dissemination of information, but now, the Chairmanship, where possible, is rotated as is the task of taking minutes. I have also encouraged staff to help/support/advise each other, mainly by remaining silent when others are perfectly happy to proffer suggestions.
2 Relationship with the Head – although I respect the Head enormously I am unsure of my position here. Where is the line to be drawn between his area of responsibility in the school and mine for the department? I now tend to seek him out on a regular weekly basis in order to keep him and me in touch. Whereas last year I would wait until there was a crisis or a problem, now the meetings are less crucial and as a consequence more helpful.

This report of a stress-reduction programme is an indication of the possibility of moving from recommendation to implementation on a small scale within a school. This model of organizational change is now available for other teams in the school to use for their own plans.

Many of the recommendations which I have discussed need the support of the LEA and I want to end this chapter by asking that much more consideration be given by teachers, advisers and administrators to the role of the LEA in strengthening organiz- ational resources. Valuable contributions are already being made by advisers and education officers. But there are further major contributions which could be made and three of them are closely related to the major recommendations in this chapter. First is the improvement of selection procedures by systematic guidance and training of professional and non-professional members of inter- viewing panels. Second is the establishment of a careers consultancy service for teachers, advisers and administrative staff which would be serviced by external consultants. Third is the provision of an integrated in-service training service for all LEA staff.

These recommendations offer indications of the many potential organizational resources which could be implemented in LEAs and schools for the reduction of stress. It is hoped they will prove strong enough to withstand current and impending pressures.

References

APPLEY, M. H. and TRUMBULL, R. (1967) *Psychological Stress*. New York: Appleton Century Crofts.

BONE, T. (1983) 'Exercising leadership' in A. Paisey (ed.) *The Effective Teacher*. Ward Lock Educational.

CARLESTAM, G. (1971) 'Planning for a good environment' in L. Levi (ed.) *Society, Stress and Disease*. Oxford: Oxford University Press.

CLWYD COUNTY COUNCIL (1976) *Absenteeism and Disruptive Behaviour*. Mold: Clwyd County Council.

COTGROVE, S., DUNHAM, J. and VAMPLEW, C. (1971) *The Nylon Spinners*. Allen & Unwin.

COX, T. (1977) 'The nature and management of stress in schools' in Clwyd County Council. *The Management of Stress in Schools*. Mold: Clwyd County Council.

DUNHAM, J. (1976) 'Stress situations and responses' in National Association of Schoolmasters/Union of Women Teachers. *Stress in Schools*. Hemel Hempstead: NAS/UWT.

——— (1980) 'An exploratory comparative study of staff stress in English and German comprehensive schools'. *Educational Review*, 32 (1).

EYSENCK, H. J. (1975) *Encyclopedia of Psychology*. Fontana.

GARDELL, B. (1971) 'Alienation and mental health in the modern industrial environment' in L. Levi (ed.) *Society, Stress and Disease*. Oxford: Oxford University Press.

HEBB, D. (1972) *Textbook of Psychology*. Philadelphia, Pennsylvania: Saunders.

KAHN, R. L. (1973) 'Conflict, ambiguity and overload: three elements in job stress'. *Occupational Mental Health*, 3 (1).

KYRIACOU, C. (1981) 'Social support and occupational stress among school teachers'. *Educational Studies*, 7 (1).

——— and SUTCLIFFE, J. (1977) 'Teacher stress: a review'. *Educational Review*, 29 (4).

MARLAND, M. and HILL, S. (1981) *Departmental Management*. Heinemann Educational Books.

MASIDLOVER, L. (1981) 'Simple 9-point plan to beat stress'. Washington: *National Enquirer*, July 14.

SELYE, H. (1974) *Stress Without Distress*. New York: Lippincott.

8 Self-evaluation

Robert McCormick

This collection starts with the skill of facilitating discussion and planning. It ends with the key managerial skill of evaluation. The autonomy of the British school and the effectiveness of the management skills developed and deployed must rest on the willingness to evaluate. We are more used to evaluation as something done to us by 'outsiders' (local education authority advisers, HM Inspectors, researchers) for their own purposes (often to tell us we are not good enough). Here we consider ways of evaluating our own work as part of our own planning and managerial process.

MM

Self-evaluation is not unfamiliar: teachers in classrooms use constant feedback from pupils as the basis for instantaneous self-evaluation. Heads of departments, deputy heads and headteachers may reflect occasionally on their role. What may be less familiar is for groups of teachers in a school to carry out a self-evaluation, in this case the 'self' is more than a single teacher. Whether familiar or not systematic forms of self-evaluation have increased in importance in recent years, particularly at the level of the whole school.

Self-evaluation can be contrasted with the more usual formal evaluations, for example, by inspectors, because the evaluator and evaluated are one and the same person (or group). The participation in, and control of, the evaluation are important aspects. Some local education authorities have initiated self-evaluation activities which honour the principles of participation but which remove the control from the teachers. They do this by the simple mechanism of requiring a report to be submitted to the Education Committee. Understandably, teachers bear this in mind when conducting the evaluation and it inevitably affects, for example, their candour. However, there exists a range of self-evaluations from the private one a teacher carries out for his/her own benefit to the 'public' one where a report goes to a body outside the school. The definition of what is truly self-evaluation is not easy but the ideas of 'participation' and 'control' will be central.

The main part of this chapter will be concerned with two elements: how to conduct self-evaluation and how to manage self-evaluation. (McCormick and James (1983) and the Open University (1982a) give fuller accounts of all forms of evaluation in schools, including self-evaluation.) Methods of evaluation are usually the same for single teachers and for groups, but the management of it is of most relevance when groups of teachers attempt a self-evaluation.

Why evaluate?

But first, why do we evaluate and why *self*-evaluation? Evaluation has been thought necessary to provide the evidence for improvements in teaching. But why is it being emphasized now, to the extent that the Oxfordshire Chief Education Officer thinks it should be part of the activity of all schools (Brighouse 1983, pp. 27 and 30)? Partly this is because of the 'accountability movement' which, though largely having disappeared, drew attention to the need for accounts of school activities to be given. For some this implied increased activity by inspectors to satisfy a legal or formal accountability for the money spent on education. This proved unacceptable. First, it was just not feasible without a massive increase in inspectors, particularly at the local level. More importantly, this approach ignores other concepts of accountability. Teachers, as professionals, see it as their job either individually or collectively to evaluate their own work, that is, a moral or professional accountability. Thus we have self-evaluation with the emphasis on professional development and educational improvement. The decline in concern for legal accountability at the LEA level, under pressure of coping with cuts in expenditure, has not been mirrored within the Department of Education and Science, as manifest in the White Paper *Teacher Quality*. Indeed this has now been reinforced in legislation on teacher appraisal (see chapter 4). Another approach is the idea of encouraging professional development as a positive response to stagnant job prospects and decreasing mobility for teachers. The idea of improvement and professional development also has other roots as expressed by Stenhouse (1975) in the 'teacher-as-researcher'. This sees the teacher as trying to build up knowledge and understanding about teaching, and was manifest in, for example, the Ford Teaching Project. There is little difference in practice between this research-based approach and that of evaluation, except that the latter may be more short-term and focus on policy making: it is decision-oriented rather than concerned with knowledge creation.

What to evaluate?

This is the first question in an evaluation. Anything can be the focus for evaluation within the school: teaching approach (for example, who does the teacher interact with in the classroom?); the school organization (for example, how information is disseminated to teachers); the school and its environment (for example, communications with parents). The problem is in deciding what to evaluate. Some evaluators advocate keeping an open mind when starting an investigation, but that can be difficult for a school which inevitably has limited resources for evaluation. In any case as insiders teachers have insights into their classrooms or schools which allow them to identify what is worthy of investigation.

The evaluation is therefore best started with an attempt to isolate a problem or issue to be studied: why is it a problem and what aspects of the school or classroom are affected? The choice of problem or issue should be based on its importance and whether or not it is tractable. The latter point is especially important in initial attempts. So, for example, a teacher carrying out a self-evaluation in the classroom would be unwise to start with the problem of resource allocation at school or departmental level, unless prepared (and able) to engage in the battle at that level. (Perhaps teachers do this rather than face what may seem like personal inadequacies.) This points also to the need to think about the kind of action that can be taken when defining the evaluation problem.

An even more directed approach is advocated by some (for example, Shipman 1979, 1983): evaluate the effectiveness of the school or teacher in achieving specified aims and objectives. This entails first creating the aims and objectives with sufficient precision to evaluate their achievement, and then secondly identifying indicators to measure achievement. For example, if it is the aim of a secondary school to ensure that all (or a maximum number of) pupils get some kind of public examination qualification, then examination results are logical indicators. The objections to this approach are obvious. Not all objectives have such evident or single indicators. For example, the aim to create a 'caring attitude' could be indicated by children being encouraged to cooperate over work, sharing ideas and materials or by politeness, etc. At a more basic level it is questionable whether aims and objectives can be drawn up and agreed upon in sufficient detail for evaluation purposes. These objections have not, however, prevented the DES from advocating the use of aims as criteria for evaluation both in Circular 6/81 and in *The School Curriculum* (DES 1981). Some schools have found that starting by drawing up a list of aims and objectives dissipates energy and enthusiasm for the evaluation. This is a problem reminiscent of the rational curriculum planning of the early curriculum development movement, though then it was small scale and less complex, not whole-school curriculum.

Many of the LEA self-evaluation schemes provide check-lists of questions to consider, covering all aspects of the school (for example,

Inner London Education Authority 1977, Oxfordshire 1979, Solihull 1979). These are intended for a wholesale review of a school. Even if the use of such a check-list is not appropriate to the particular evaluation being planned, it may be useful in selecting an agenda of issues or areas for evaluation.

Having initially defined the focus of evaluation, evaluators may be reluctant to change direction. Thus a teacher who initially sets out to evaluate his/her own questioning technique and the pupils' responses to it, may ignore the way pupils' expectations of questions are formed in other classrooms. In this case the focus may be too narrow, and evaluators must be prepared to reformulate the problem during the evaluation in the light of the evidence. This change may be a gradual one; what is referred to as progressive focusing – a refining of the focus of study. Although it is important to remain open to such changes, it is unwise to start aimlessly by, say, recording and transcribing any classroom talk. Think first what might be of interest, which classes or pupils.

How to evaluate

When schools embark on a self-evaluation it is the methods and techniques of evaluation that are given least attention. A typical approach is to assemble a group of teachers for one or two meetings and to produce a report, without any thought of conducting an investigation in the classroom, for example. An evaluation based on teacher discussion is an obvious start because teachers are an immense data source which can be drawn on in the discussion. However, this approach is also taken because teachers are by and large unfamiliar with social investigation and the importance of collecting data, or when familiar they lack the time to do it. Both of these approaches are legitimate and can be elaborated into three kinds of evaluation:

1 Teacher reflection: the teacher as a source of data, based on experience, systematically reflecting on this experience, while recognizing the limitations inherent in considering only the teacher's perspective.

2 Empirical evaluation: this recognizes that either the teachers have insufficient experience (data) relevant to an issue, or realize that they have access to a limited conception and must therefore collect data to illuminate the issue. For example, teachers are often unaware of just how much time they spend talking in the classroom and data on this may be useful.

3 Intrinsic evaluation: questions of utility or worth of what pupils experience concern values, and cannot be answered by data collection alone. Thus when reviewing the curriculum it is possible to ask 'Is what we offer worthwhile?' or 'What should we

offer?' An intrinsic evaluation is advocated by the HMI in their curriculum review exercises in conjunction with LEAs (DES 1983).

These three are not exclusive categories and they may all be necessary within an evaluation. Indeed (1) and (3) are similar in their mode of conduct in that they both require teacher discussion (assuming that it is a school or department level activity). The choice of which method to use depends on the nature of the problem or issue being evaluated, the stage reached in the evaluation and the resources available in time, energy and skills for conducting an investigation. It is important to start cautiously.

Teacher reflection

This encompasses (1) and (3) above. Take, for example, the teacher who wants to be more systematic about the reflection already carried out as part of teaching. If the topic being evaluated is how pupils work in groups, then the teacher could observe what pupils say and do as he/she goes round the class. The teacher can make cryptic notes in class or spend a few minutes after a lesson writing down anything relevant that comes to mind. These 'field' notes can be elaborated later, and can include a record of pupil (and teacher) behaviour as well as comments on that behaviour. For example:

> Sally working on own; David, Jane and Brian collaborating on prehistoric village task. *Sally doesn't usually work on her own like this; it must be because she argued with David yesterday.*

The comment is in italics to distinguish it from observation. This could have been added later, and can use past experience about pupils (*'Sally doesn't usually'*). Distinguishing observation and comment allows the teacher to check interpretations. It may be that the teacher in the above case always sees cooperative behaviour being affected by the pupils' moods, rather than, say, the nature of the task. There may be any number of reasons why Sally did not work with the others, and the teacher should be open to other possible explanations.

The detail and elaboration of the field notes will depend on the time available, but it is best to set aside whatever time can be afforded and do only what is possible in that time. Over a number of weeks such notes and reflections can be reviewed and general ideas on cooperative work developed. If, indeed, it is dependent on pupils' moods how can these be taken into account to ensure the pupils' maximum involvement in the work? Or is Sally's kind of behaviour sufficiently rare not to worry about it? Any subsequent changes in the classroom can be monitored by the same process. The amount of observational data recorded may be small, provided the reflections are systematic. Emphasizing the observations can be a second stage, that is, empirical evaluation. Indeed, it would be quite legitimate to record the reflections in the form of a diary which traces them over a period of time: thoughts stimulated by the day's events, which may themselves not be recorded in detail. Periodically reviewing the diary will allow the teacher to see his/her thoughts being formed and developing over time.

Such an approach may help the teacher to become more sensitive to events in the classroom and to think about certain issues when planning work or choosing material, etc. It could work equally well for headteachers and heads of departments if they keep a diary of their activities and reflect on them at the end of the day or week.

The problem for a teacher evaluating alone is countering bias in his/her reflections and this may require more empirical data to be collected. For teachers working as a group (a department or school) the lack of a careful recording of behaviour is less of a problem (though still a problem) because the differing experience of teachers can act as a check on the judgements of individuals. Just as individual teacher reflection needs to be systematic, so with group reflection. Unfortunately, teachers, like other professionals, are rarely self-conscious about 'discussion' and how they work together (Moon 1981). In addition teachers vary in their experience of formal discussions with colleagues, depending on their school's organization and their personal inclination to participate. Case studies of school evaluations reveal that even within one secondary school, departments will all differ in the way they set about collective reflection.

What is important is that the discussion (called 'deliberation' by some) should be orderly. For example, if a group is discussing how behavioural problems are dealt with in the school, they should not start by suggesting the required changes in the system. How does it work? What are the problems with it? These are the first questions. When possible alternative changes are considered, arguments to justify them need to be delineated and a range of alternatives specified, and alternatives which solve the problem identified. It is possible to idealize the orderly nature of this deliberation in the following steps:

1 Problem identification and definition. This should include an elaboration of the problem from the teachers' experience. For example, what are the effects in the classroom of having to go to an 'outsider' to deal with severe behaviour problems only after the lesson is over? Several anecdotes could be collected reflecting the range of experience of teachers present.
2 A consideration of various proposals for action. It is important to consider a range so as not to get hooked on single solutions.
3 For each proposal, detail the arguments for and against, including the implications for implementation. Attempt to be even-handed with each proposal.
4 Decide on the course of action.

Naturally these may not be distinct stages but some idea of progression should exist. It may also be that the group feel that they do not have sufficient data on which to discuss either the problem or its solution, and so they would start an empirical inquiry before going on to steps 2, 3 or 4.

Teachers need to develop the skills for this kind of deliberation as well as those associated with any kind of meeting: fixing times and agendas, writing up reports of proceedings and of proposals, commenting on these proposals, chairing a meeting to ensure participation and a sense of direction (as discussed in Chapters 1 and 2).

As indicated earlier, a review of the curriculum as an intrinsic evaluation can also involve teacher reflection. Both the DES and HMI (DES 1977, 1981, 1983) have encouraged and supported curriculum review exercises with the following elements:

1 Creating or reviewing statements of aims and objectives for the whole school and, in secondary schools, the ways in which departmental aims are consistent with the school's.
2 Analysing the concepts, skills and attitudes that are taught or encouraged in the school. (In a primary school this can be done by each teacher; in a secondary school at the level of a department.)
3 Analysing the curriculum to determine the extent to which areas of experience (aesthetic and creative, ethical, linguistic, mathematical, scientific, physical, social and political, spiritual) are covered. Primary-school teachers could thus see what topics and activities contributed to the aesthetic experience of their pupils.
4 Analysing the curriculum to see the extent to which particular aspects are covered, for example, preparation for working life or multi-ethnic society.

Schools are now required to provide information for parents and are encouraged by DES Circular 6/81 to produce a statement of aims. Not only can this statement be reviewed, but it can be used as a set of criteria to judge what is included in the curriculum. Questions can be posed such as: 'In what ways is this aim achieved?' or 'How does this activity satisfy the aims?' As already noted this kind of exercise can dissipate energy and seem fruitless, a problem also with the analysis of concepts, etc. ((2) above), particularly because they both generate lots of paper. Although the pay-off may be low, there is no doubt that such an analysis of concepts, etc., can reveal overlaps or gaps which exist across the curriculum, for example, across departments or years. Thus cohesion and continuity can be determined. All this, however, presupposes some idea of what is desirable, and requires more precision and detail than is found in a statement of aims. The exercises conducted by LEAs and HMI concerning the curriculum used eight 'areas of experience' as a check-list and for each subject area a department is expected to indicate the extent to which each area is covered. The rating which measures the extent is not in itself important, but the staff dicussion in arriving at it is. Experience shows that teachers need time to absorb the concepts implicit in these 'areas'. A more fundamental problem, not usually referred to, is the treatment of conflict arising from discussions of basic educational ideas. It is inevitable that teachers will exhibit different fundamental stances (ideologies). For example, some see knowledge as of prime importance in determining the curriculum; others take a more 'child-centured' approach. Review exercises which attempt to reach consensus may gloss over different and perhaps irreconcilable views. The Schools Council (1983) presented an array of frameworks for analysis as if they were either all of equal value or could all be used simultaneously, thereby ignoring ideological conflicts. This is not to say that these conflicts are easily dealt with, only that they should be recognized and tolerated. The ideologies among the staff may cover a narrower range than that held by governors, parents and others involved with the school, but the views of these 'outsiders' will increasingly be important.

Curriculum review as depicted so far is what the Schools Council (1983) described as, 'aims to practice' (intrinsic evaluation). It can equally be of the form 'practice to aims', and thus, some would argue, less woolly and rooted more in the realities of the classroom. This does not necessarily mean an empirical evaluation, as teacher deliberation is still appropriate, the teacher being the data source. Some schools have nevertheless undertaken empirical work by, for example, a shadow study – that is, following one or more pupils around the school to observe their total curriculum experience. For a number of days a teacher sits in all the lessons and observes all the activities carried out by the pupils under observation as well as the general class activities. Here is an instance when it is not possible to distinguish evaluations as clearly empirical or intrinsic.

Empirical evaluation

The shadow study and the field notes used in individual teacher reflection are both examples of empirical methods. These methods have a tradition in social science research which is concerned about being rigorous in collecting and analysing data, and in forming conclusions – that is, in avoiding bias. The conclusions may aim to create more knowledge about a phenomena, whereas evaluation is primarily concerned with action, but the rigours of this research tradition are no less important although unfamiliar to many teachers. They are concerned with validity (observing what we say is being observed) and reliability (consistently observing it). Avoiding bias is particularly important for the individual teacher's self-evaluation and collecting empirical data can help to distance the teacher from his/her perceptions of teaching. This is no less important for a group of teachers. The care with which researchers employ techniques of investigation cannot be emulated by busy teachers and the advice and methods given here try to take this into account.

Audio recording

Audio recording is a relatively simple method of obtaining classroom data, particularly on teacher behaviour. The easiest method is for the teacher to carry a cassette recorder (with built-in microphone) on a shoulder strap. Obviously this is selective and focuses on the teacher's talk and that of surrounding pupils. If 'teacher talk' is not the prime focus of study, the recording can be used to reconstruct the whole lesson, by recording observations and comments at the end of the lesson as suggested earlier with field notes. This may be necessary if non-verbal behaviour is important. When pupil behaviour is the focus, especially when not initiated directly by the teacher, then a group of pupils can be recorded by placing a recorder among them. This is particularly appropriate in primary schools where children are in groups around tables. In secondary schools it can be used, for example, to record pupil–pupil interaction in the laboratory.

Recording in the classroom requires trials and experimentation. First the pupils, and indeed the teacher, must become used to the presence of a recorder so that their behaviour is not too abnormal. Carrying the recorder around for some time before actually recording allows pupils to settle down. Secondly, to obtain a quality recording will need experimentation in positioning the recorder and microphone, and perhaps even in using different equipment. The recording is unlikely to be perfect and a balance must be struck between the quality and the trouble involved and the obtrusiveness of the equipment.

The real headache with audio recording is what to do with the resulting tapes. Transcription of a whole lesson in longhand will take around ten times the length of the lesson (seven hours!), and then there is the analysis. So some short cuts are necessary. Listen to the tape and pick out significant incidents for detailed transcription; or roughly transcribe the whole lesson, but not in detail, and then pick out specific incidents. Alternatively the tape may not be transcribed but used as a stimulus for teacher reflection. The nature of the analysis, whether transcribed or not, is more difficult to prescribe. Obviously if the focus for the evaluation is clear, the analysis will be too. For instance, a teacher may be concerned about what kinds of extended interactions he/she has with his/her pupils. These can be selected and categorized in terms of, say, the type and depth of concepts discussed, or the kinds of pupil responses – a qualitative analysis. On the other hand, a quantitative analysis may be appropriate where teachers want to know if they spend longer talking to boys than to girls, or to 'bright' rather than to 'slow' pupils.

Observation

Observation of a teacher's lesson can be carried out by a trusted colleague or outsider. This allows a wider range of information to be recorded than using an audio-cassette, although if both are used then the observer and observed can share a common set of data. An observer in the classroom may note down either the occurrence of pre-specified behaviour, or simply what he/she thinks is significant. The use of an audio recording helps the observed teacher challenge this choice. Noting pre-specified behaviour may be a relatively mechanical and neutral task and, if the categories are simple, can even be done by a pupil – for example, recording the times teacher speaks in French rather than English in a language lesson. More often than not the observer's decisions will require discussion with the teacher. This can only happen if there is a good relationship between them, otherwise the observer will seem threatening, something I return to later.

Interviewing pupils

Interviewing pupils provides quite different kind of data from the techniques described above, which give either teacher or pupil behaviour and lead to teacher's perceptions and reflections on that behaviour. Interviewing allows the pupils' perceptions and meanings to be ascertained. Pupils can be interviewed about specific lessons and their views on certain events within these, prompted perhaps by an audio recording. More usually the teacher will want the pupils' general views about the teaching, the curriculum area, the subject or the school. Not only do interviews give access to pupil perceptions but also to data on events which cannot be observed by the teacher, particularly important when investigating the hidden curriculum of the classroom and the school.

Interviewing is a deceptively simple technique. For teachers the problems are more acute than for outside researchers. This is because the teachers change role when interviewing and have to make this clear to the pupils. The teacher does not want, for example, compliant or 'correct' answers – what the pupils think are required. Also the authority the teacher has in class should not extend to the interview, a question I return to when discussing ethics. A teacher needs to be particularly sensitive to the pupils so that they feel at ease and able to talk frankly about delicate or difficult issues. Like other aspects of interviewing, such as questioning technique, setting the atmosphere is a skill that must be learnt, and teachers should not feel too disappointed if initial attempts are unsuccessful. One way of taking the pressure off individual pupils, and conducting an interview in a more familiar context, is to do it with a group.

Unless the language or expression of ideas by pupils is being analysed it is not advisable to record the interviews. An audio recording may be a useful back-up if the notes taken during an interview are unclear, but the effort of transcription will rarely pay off. In addition the recorder may inhibit pupils. Notes are in any case an essential discipline for the interviewer, allowing him/her to keep track of the progress of the interview, recording questions to return to later and, most important, providing a preliminary analysis. As with audio recording analysis it depends on the focus of the evaluation, which is in turn reflected in the kind of interview. More particularly the type of interview depends on the questions asked: a clear focus leads to specific questions and hence a structured interview. It is more usual to employ a semi-structured or unstructured interview where only general issues are borne in mind by the interviewer; the pupil responses determine the progression of the interview. Unstructured interviews, attractive in their potential for providing 'in-depth' information, are very difficult to conduct well.

Questionnaires

Questionnaires are probably the most misused form of data collection. The lack of direct contact between the data collector (interviewer) and respondent (interviewee) has to be made up for by sensitive visual design and scrupulous attention to question wording. Lots of advice is available so it is worth reading it up before plunging in (for example, Youngman, undated). The advantage of questionnaires over interviews is that they can be answered anonymously. This is important in encouraging pupils to give candid views on what happens in the classroom or school. They also allow a wider sample of pupils to be tapped. This is a form of economy of effort, but it is at the expense of the potential depth of an interview. Questionnaires can be more or less structured, as with interviews, though in the former the questioner cannot probe pupil responses. A completely unstructured 'questionnaire' might be an invitation to pupils to write any kind of comment on a lesson, or lessons over a term or year. This may be easy to design but it is difficult and time-consuming to analyse. It is a good discipline to consider how the questionnaire will be analysed before designing it. This saves much trouble later.

Assessment data

By assessment data I mean the information collected on pupil performance on such things as tests, examinations, project work and homework. The data from these are primarily designed to assess individual pupils, but quite clearly if a test shows that many do not understand a specific concept or idea, teachers could then take this as a problem in the teaching and try to change their approach. This use of routine assessment information for evaluation, is not unfamiliar to many. The more specialized task of designing assessment procedures specifically to evaluate a teaching approach is not likely to be worth the effort, and it is better to rely on existing procedures.

A basic idea in assessment is the referencing system. Public examinations have a roughly fixed percentage of passes and fails and are therefore norm-referenced, with the 'norm' being set by all those who sit the examination. Graded tests on the other hand give scores based on how well pupils meet specific criteria, that is, they are criterion-referenced. On the face of it this kind of assessment is best for evaluation, for failings in the teaching can be pinpointed by failure to meet certain criteria – for example, an error analysis of the ideas in pupil essays or the distractors (incorrect options) chosen in a multiple-choice question. Profiles, which record achievement on a variety of aspects of learning, can be used to see where weaknesses occur by identifying those aspects on which a high proportion of pupils fail to do well. Essays, multiple-choice questions and profiles are constructed or set by teachers and are directly related to their teaching, therefore an analysis of problems is a good reflection of that teaching. Graded tests, though originating outside the school, can still be used for evaluation, providing teachers are satisfied that they assess what they teach (that is, that the tests have content validity).

The most notable forms of norm-referenced assessment are those originating outside the school: public examinations and standardized tests. They only provide general information about the teaching in a particular area. A school finding that the CSE or O-level passes in mathematics are lower one year than in the previous may wonder if the teaching is at fault (assuming that the general standards of the national examination population and the school candidates were the same as their respective predecessors the year before). Only further investigation will establish the cause of the decline in passes. Many kinds of comparisons are possible and the Open University (1982b), Shipman (1979) and McCormick and James (1983) give guidance on these.

Summary
In theory all the above techniques can be used for individual or group self-evaluation, although most experience has been with individual teachers. Audio recording with its focus on fine detail is generally of more use to individuals, whereas observation can serve both individuals and groups. For groups the observation will be global (for example, a shadow study) or pre-specified (for example, the time teachers spend talking to boys rather than girls). Interviews and questionnaires are also useful for both. Classroom assessment procedures are of more use to individual teachers, with norm-referenced procedures being appropriate at school level (where in any case more resources are available for analysis).

Issues

The attention given above to why, what and how to evaluate provides only the most general guide to organizing an evaluation. There is no simple sequence of steps to guide an evaluator through. Nevertheless it is possible to give some pointers.

Most important is time. Teachers rarely have enough time and often cannot get it at the right moment, therefore evaluation activities must be set to fit the time available. If time can be made available from timetable time this is even better. Whatever is available must be set aside and adhered to; if the school or department think it important then it should not be shoved to one side. Just as important as the amount of time available is the time of the year when it occurs. Different schools, and the teachers within them, have different cycles of activity. Evaluation needs to fit into these cycles, and this is sometimes best when teachers are apparently busiest, but with maximum energy – that is, in the autumn rather than the end of the summer term. Both the amount of time and the timing will circumscribe the size of the evaluation task. Initially, modest amounts of time should be allocated and an incremental approach rather than a whole-school evaluation adopted. For a single teacher, isolating one aspect of his/her teaching will be more manageable to start with. Larger evaluations can be built up by cyclic or periodic investigations, taking, say, one aspect of the school each time.

Then there are the evaluation skills. Evaluators cannot expect to be able to employ sophisticated data-gathering techniques. In the early stages particularly, it is better for teachers to develop skills they already have, such as discussion and deliberation, and then move on to simple empirical methods. So observation could be based on everyday approaches but done more self-consciously and systematically, before progressing to audio recording. A start can be made by writing down anecdotes of events in the classroom. During these early stages evaluators need not be too concerned about the traditions of researchers, but rather be aware of bias; for example, are there alternative interpretations to explain what has been observed?

One important aid to both the problem of lack of skills and of bias is the use of an outsider. If a school is undertaking an evaluation then an adviser or a local college lecturer may help in developing skills. The outsider could go one step further and actually directly provide the skills by, say, interviewing pupils. This provides some measure of independence (reducing bias caused by a teacher's presence in the interview) and will give another perspective. For an individual teacher doing a self-evaluation another teacher acting as a critical friend (as suggested earlier) will be helpful. There are also examples of teachers using the pupils themselves to interview each other!

But the use of outsiders, particularly when observing classrooms, usually raises another issue, that of threat. The most threatening situation is when an inspector observes and, though this does not happen in a self-evaluation, senior staff may have the same effect. Even if senior staff do not actually observe, the power they have over junior staff careers is sufficient for them to constitute a threat. Thus if teachers are being interviewed, or writing a report on their work for those above them, they may be less candid. They can also feel threatened when it comes to implementing changes required as a result of evaluation. To allay this fear teachers should participate in, and control, the evaluation. Not only is this a democratic principle, it also improves the effectiveness of any changes that are implemented. Teachers would understandably resist something they felt was the result of a process they had little to do with, simply a senior management (or headteacher) affair.

Being sensitive to the threat an evaluation may pose may mean that confidentiality (about, say, what happens in a teacher's classroom) may have to be respected. This raises an ethical issue. On the one hand, to encourage teachers to participate it may be necessary to respect their privacy, but on the other, this denies others the right to know when something is amiss. The unequal power relation between a teacher and senior staff compounds this problem, because the information can be used against the teacher. There is no easy resolution to this conflict of interest, and until the staff are familiar with evaluation and feel more confident about it, it is better to err on the side of respecting the privacy of the teacher.

The above problems can be accommodated by the following procedures in organizing a school evaluation:

1 Initially all staff should be consulted and should approve the evaluation and the procedures for it. (Do not mislead them about the real purpose: if it is to weed out ineffectual staff do not disguise this; self-evaluation is to help develop the staff.)

2 Keep everyone informed as it progresses, especially those who are not centrally involved.

3 Try to ensure a maximum number of staff are involved, and that there is a mix of levels of staff.

4 Respect data confidentiality. Specifically allow teachers to check what is recorded about them and clear what will be reported about them. (This is inhibiting, but necessary for a true self-evaluation. If it is anything less then the procedures must be agreed with the staff.)

5 Negotiate with teachers how the report will be used and to whom it will be circulated.

6 Practise reciprocity – if junior teachers are being evaluated so must senior staff be, not just as classroom teachers but as headteachers, deputies, etc.

These procedures assume that staff meet and particpate in decision-making, something which may be foreign to the organizational style of the school. It is perhaps a truism to say that this organizational style will be reflected in the evaluation, and an attempt to adopt the kinds of procedures advocated above may conflict with this style.

Pupils may also feel threatened. Of course, ultimately the pupils should benefit from the evaluation, but they may be less candid if they feel their rights are being violated. Teachers usually assume they have the right to control information concerning pupils (for example, an audio recording of a lesson), but this simply transfers a right as a teacher to that as an evaluator. Usually pupils also assume the teacher has the right to such information, but teachers must be careful to act in the pupils' interests. Even if the child does not object, the parents may. The individual teacher doing an evaluation has to be aware of the effect outside his/her classroom.

The kinds of procedures outlined are likely to mean an important role for senior staff. In a whole-school evaluation (or one which tackles a school-wide issue) there will be a need to coordinate the activities. Senior staff must also facilitate its operation by giving access to data, making time for meetings, supporting the production of a report and, eventually, by implementing the results. The concomitant effect of this role for senior staff is overload, particularly when data are being collated and analysed and a report written. This reinforces the advice on controlling the size of the evaluation. In planning the evaluation, therefore, the load should be spread among the staff, and over time.

Reporting a whole-school evaluation often causes excessive workloads because the writer(s) has no firm view of its purpose. This leads to overlong reports ('must put in everything we collected'), lacking both in focus and critical views. Mandatory self-evaluations often suffer from bland and boring reports indicating a ritualistic response. For a school undertaking an evaluation the report may:

1 Educate all the staff (not just those involved) and sensitize them to issues about which they can take individual action.
2 Convince staff of the need to take action and change individual or school procedures, activities, etc.
3 Lay out proposals for change with justification from the data, which can form the basis of staff discussion about change.

There is a distinct difference between the last two: (2) need not propose changes but simply be an initial input to the earlier deliberations, whereas (3) is at a more advanced stage. Evaluation, and the reporting of it in particular, is a form of learning. The format of the report should reflect the way in which the audience can best learn. Science staff may welcome pages of statistics, but others may find a qualitative description of a classroom incident more enlightening. What of the individual teacher's self-evaluation? Who is the audience and what purpose can a report serve? Assuming that the teacher is acting alone, a report may indeed be unnecessary; the learning will have taken place during the evaluation and thinking about it. But it can serve a purpose as a check on validity. The formalizing of the data and actions for change to an imaginary audience as it were may help a teacher guard against unwarranted assumptions and bias.

Change

Reporting is sometimes seen as the final stage of an evaluation, but the above discussion sees it as leading into decision-making and, if necessary, change. This is the logic of starting with a problem in need of solution. But sometimes evaluations 'fail' because the decision-making processes within the school cannot cope. In particular, schools whose organization is fragmented have difficulty in dealing with evaluations which address cross-school issues. Heads of departments meetings may be preoccupied with defending patches rather than with cross-school changes. Such problems of implementation take us back to initial decisions about the evaluation: at what level should it be conducted? Those who advocate individual teacher self-evaluation see change as taking place from the classroom upwards. Everyone will acknowledge that teachers meet obstacles to change that lie outside the classroom, and so some advocate starting at a school level. Both approaches may be needed, but the lesson is that evaluation is a process of change and how change takes place must be considered for each evaluation in the specific context of a school. As many schools and individual teachers have found, change through evaluation is not always a rational sequential process (problem identification, data collection, analysis and proposals for action). The learning essential for change may be as a consequence of involvement in the process rather than in the elegance of the results.

Conclusion

At this point let me return to a consideration of the nature of self-evaluation. I started by noting that there is a range of kinds, and throughout have stressed the particpation of staff in all types. The justifications for this stance are: it is democratic; it aids change by making teachers a party to decisions; it aids change by involvement in the learning process. On these grounds some writers discount LEA initiated self-evaluation. They argue that the power of the LEA to sanction the school is not conducive to self-evaluation. But within a school such a situation also exists, which would imply that only individual teachers, in the privacy of their own classroom, can self-evaluate. Even here it is not simple as my discussion of the rights of pupils indicated. At all levels confidentiality is important, and the degree of it will depend on the amount of trust that exists among the various parties.

This approach is justified (in the face of demands for inspection, for example) in the name of professional development and the improvement of education. It is as well, however, to remember that it is but one strategy. Schools will be subjected to other kinds and self-evaluation should not be advocated as a form of protectionism. Like other strategies evaluation must be seen as a long-term activity. To reiterate, this implies: gradually evaluating parts of school or classroom activity, not all of it at once; progressively developing the skills of evaluation (for example, data collection); encouraging and improving methods of teachers working together; ensuring that the structures for change exist within the school at all levels. Evaluation is a relative newcomer to the repertoire of professional teachers and one which does not always follow naturally from classroom teaching skills. As such it needs time and practice to develop, and thought about its effectiveness.

References

BRIGHOUSE, T. (1983) 'A glimpse of the future – what sort of society do we want?' in M. Galton and B. Moon (eds) *Changing Schools . . . Changing Curriculum*. Harper & Row.

DES (1977) *Curriculum 11-16* (Working Papers by HMI). HMSO.

DES (1981) *The School Curriculum*. HMSO.

DES (1983) *Curriculum 11-16: Towards a Statement of Entitlement*. HMSO.

INNER LONDON EDUCATION AUTHORITY (1977) *Keeping the School under Review*. ILEA.

MCCORMICK, R. and JAMES, M. (1983) *Curriculum Evaluation in Schools*. Croom Helm.

MOON, B. (1981) 'Curriculum research: agenda for the eighties'. Paper presented at SSRC Seminar 7-9 January.

OPEN UNIVERSITY (1982a) *E364: Curriculum Evaluation and Assessment in Educational Institutions*. Milton Keynes: Open University Press.

——— (1982b) *Making More Sense of Examination Results*. Milton Keynes: Open University Press.

OXFORDSHIRE EDUCATION COMMITTEE (1979) *Starting Points in Self-evaluation*.

SCHOOLS COUNCIL (1983) *Primary Practice: a Sequal to 'The Practical Curriculum'*. Methuen Educational.

SHIPMAN, M. (1979) *In-school Evaluation*, Heinemann Educational Books.

———— (1983) *Assessment in Primary and Middle Schools*. Croom Helm.

SOLIHULL LEA (1979) *Evaluating the School – a Guide for Secondary Schools in the Metropolitan Borough of Solihull*.

STENHOUSE, L. (1975) *An Introduction to Curriculum Research and Development*. Heinemann Educational Books.

YOUNGMAN, M.B. (undated) *Designing and Analysing Questionnaires*. Rediguide 12. University of Nottingham, School of Education.

(Many of the ideas here developed out of work on a book with Mary James (McCormick and James 1983) and I am indebted to her and other colleagues at the Open University for their help and support.)

Further Reading

This is a short list of books recommended for those in schools who are anxious to develop their school management skills. It is *not*, of course, an attempt at a full bibliography.

A recent full bibliography on school management with a wide range is Douglas J. Thom's *A Teaching Bibliography for Educational Administration*, issue 33 (March 1984) of *Studies in Education Administration*, Commonwealth Council for Educational Administration. Shorter bibliographies can be found in many of the books listed.

BARRY, C.H. and TYE, F. (1972) *Running a School*. Maurice Temple Smith.

BLACKBURN, K. (1983) *Head of House, Head of Year*. Heinemann Educational Books.

BOLAM, R. (1982) *School-Focussed In-Service Training*. Heinemann Educational Books.

JOHN, D. (1980) *Leadership in School*. Heinemann Educational Books.

KNIGHT, B. (1983) *Managing School Finance*. Heinemann Educational Books.

LYONS, G. (1976) *Head's Tasks*. Windsor: NFER Publishing (now NFER-Nelson).

MARLAND, M. (1971) *Head of Department*. Heinemann Educational Books.

——— and HILL, S. (1981) *Departmental Management*. Heinemann Educational Books.

OPEN UNIVERSITY (1981) *Management and the School*. Milton Keynes: Open University Press.

PAISEY, A. (ed.) (1984) *Jobs in Schools*. Heinemann Educational Books.

POSTER, C. (1976) *School Decision-Making*. Heinemann Educational Books.

RICHARDSON, E. (1973) *The Teacher, the School and the Task of Management*. Heinemann Educational Books.

WATERS, D. (1983) *Responsibility and Promotion in the Primary School*. Heinemann Educational Books.
WHITAKER, P. (1983) *The Primary Head*. Heinemann Educational Books.

Contributors

COLIN BAYNE-JARDINE was Headmaster of Culverhay School, Bath, for six years prior to taking up his present post as Headmaster of Henbury School, Bristol, in 1976. In 1969 he was appointed a school-based tutor by Bristol University and was one of the early professional tutors. He has also taught in the USA, Canada, Glasgow, and Devon. As well as volumes on Mussolini and the Second World War in the Longman's Modern Times Series, he has written about the study and teaching of history, and contributed a chapter to *Departmental Management* (Heinemann Educational Books 1981).

KEITH BLACKBURN is Head of St George's School, Gravesend. From 1976 until 1982 he was Deputy Head of Altwood School, Maidenhead, with responsibility for the curriculum, and before that Head of House at Crown Woods, a large comprehensive school in south-east London. He has wide experience of pastoral care and counselling, and frequently lectures and runs courses on pastoral care. He devised the National Book League exhibition, 'Pastoral Care in Action'. In 1982 he helped to establish the National Association of Pastoral Care in Education of which he is the Vice-Chair. Keith Blackburn was ordained as an Anglican priest in 1964 and he continues to combine his school and other work with church duties. As well as journal articles he has written *The Tutor* (Heinemann Educational Books 1975) and *Head of House, Head of Year* (Heinemann Educational Books 1983).

LESLEY BULMAN is Headteacher of Kingsdale School, ILEA, after having been Deputy Head at Abbey Wood School in south London. After gaining a B.Sc. in biochemistry at the London Medical School and professional training at the London Institute of Education, she taught chemistry, being Head of Science Department in two comprehensive schools. She has written in the NAPCE journal *Pastoral Care*, the book *Teaching Language and Study Skills in Secondary Science* (Heinemann Educational Books 1985) and, with David Jenkins, the forthcoming *The Pastoral Curriculum* (Basil Blackwell).

JACK DUNHAM, B.Sc., M.Ed., Ph.D., Dip.Psy., started his career as a teacher at a grammar school and then held posts in two secondary schools and a primary school. He eventually became Head of Ardwick Remedial Centre in Manchester. Dr Dunham then became a child psychologist in Bristol and later had a training appointment with the Bristol Aeroplane Company. His research interests for a number of years have been concerned with stress in social work and educational settings, on which he has written and run courses. He is now a tutor in Further Professional Studies at the the School of Education, University of Bristol.

LAURIE GOODHAND is Head of Quintin Kynaston School in Inner London. After a B.Sc. in chemistry from Imperial College, London, and professional training at Leicester University and Keele University (where he studied counselling), he taught in the Midlands and at Holland Park School, London (where he was Head of Department and a Pastoral Head). He is joint author of the ILEA *Study Skills* book for pupils (1984).

IAN LESLIE, after an Honours Degree in modern and medieval languages, joined the then London County Council in the Administrative Grade, and has worked for it and later, the Inner London Education Authority, ever since in many branches from School Bus Service through Learning Resources (equipment supply), Teachers' Pay, etc., to his present post of School Secretary, Stoke Newington School. While in further education central management, he participated in the introduction of 'visible index' FE college student records – the paper precursor of the present-day microcomputer-stored databases. He was formerly Chairman, National Committee for Legalisation of Citizens' Band Radio and Vice-President of European CB Federation; at present he is President of British Citizens' Band Council.

ROBERT McCORMICK is a senior lecturer at the School of Education at the Open University. He has been at the Open University for thirteen years: four years in the Institute of Educational Technology working with course teams in the Technology Faculty; eight years in the Faculty (and now the School) of Education. He has worked on courses in the area of curriculum studies and recently was course team chair of 'Curriculum Evaluation and Assessment in Education Institutions'. Currently he is working on courses in the area of technology in schools. His research interests are in evaluation in schools and particularly self-evaluation, including collaborative research with teachers. Recent publications: *Calling Education to Account* (ed.) (Heinemann Educational Books 1982) and *Curriculum Evaluation in Schools* with Mary James (Croom Helm 1983).

MICHAEL MARLAND, before becoming Headmaster of North

Westminster Community School in January 1980, was Headmaster of Woodberry Down School, London, for nine years. Prior to that, most of his teaching experience was in large London comprehensive schools. He was a member of the Bullock Committee, Chairman of the Schools Council English Committee, and the National Book League's Use of Books in Schools Working Party. As well as being a frequent broadcaster and lecturer on a wide range of educational issues, he is general editor of the Heinemann Organization in Schools Series. His numerous publications include *Language Across the Curriculum* (Heineman Educational Books 1977) and *Sex Differentiation and Schooling* (Heinemann Educational Books 1983). He was awarded the CBE for services to education in the Queen's Silver Jubilee Honours List and made Honorary Professor of Education at Warwick University in 1980. He is currently chair of the National Association for Pastoral Care in Education, The National Textbook Reference Library Steering Committee, and the Royal Opera House Education Advisory Council.

GEORGE PHIPSON, before becoming Head of West Hatch High School, Essex, was Deputy Head responsible for curriculum and timetabling at Abbey Wood School, London, and previously Head of Mathematics and Senior Teacher: In-Service Training at Woodberry Down School, and a teacher of mathematics at Bristol Grammar School. As well as lecturing on timetabling, he has contributed to *School-Focussed In-Service Training* (Heinemann Educational Books 1982) edited by Ray Bolam and *Departmental Management* (Heinemann Educational Books 1981).

Index